PROJECT BIOSHIELD: CONTRACTING FOR THE HEALTH AND SECURITY OF THE AMERICAN PUBLIC

HEARING

BEFORE THE

COMMITTEE ON GOVERNMENT REFORM

HOUSE OF REPRESENTATIVES

ONE HUNDRED EIGHTH CONGRESS

FIRST SESSION

APRIL 4, 2003

Serial No. 108–10

Printed for the use of the Committee on Government Reform

Available via the World Wide Web: http://www.gpo.gov/congress/house
http://www.house.gov/reform

U.S. GOVERNMENT PRINTING OFFICE

87–141 PDF WASHINGTON : 2003

For sale by the Superintendent of Documents, U.S. Government Printing Office
Internet: bookstore.gpo.gov Phone: toll free (866) 512–1800; DC area (202) 512–1800
Fax: (202) 512–2250 Mail: Stop SSOP, Washington, DC 20402–0001

COMMITTEE ON GOVERNMENT REFORM

TOM DAVIS, Virginia, *Chairman*

DAN BURTON, Indiana
CHRISTOPHER SHAYS, Connecticut
ILEANA ROS-LEHTINEN, Florida
JOHN M. McHUGH, New York
JOHN L. MICA, Florida
MARK E. SOUDER, Indiana
STEVEN C. LaTOURETTE, Ohio
DOUG OSE, California
RON LEWIS, Kentucky
JO ANN DAVIS, Virginia
TODD RUSSELL PLATTS, Pennsylvania
CHRIS CANNON, Utah
ADAM H. PUTNAM, Florida
EDWARD L. SCHROCK, Virginia
JOHN J. DUNCAN, Jr., Tennessee
JOHN SULLIVAN, Oklahoma
NATHAN DEAL, Georgia
CANDICE S. MILLER, Michigan
TIM MURPHY, Pennsylvania
MICHAEL R. TURNER, Ohio
JOHN R. CARTER, Texas
WILLIAM J. JANKLOW, South Dakota
MARSHA BLACKBURN, Tennessee

HENRY A. WAXMAN, California
TOM LANTOS, California
MAJOR R. OWENS, New York
EDOLPHUS TOWNS, New York
PAUL E. KANJORSKI, Pennsylvania
CAROLYN B. MALONEY, New York
ELIJAH E. CUMMINGS, Maryland
DENNIS J. KUCINICH, Ohio
DANNY K. DAVIS, Illinois
JOHN F. TIERNEY, Massachusetts
WM. LACY CLAY, Missouri
DIANE E. WATSON, California
STEPHEN F. LYNCH, Massachusetts
CHRIS VAN HOLLEN, Maryland
LINDA T. SANCHEZ, California
C.A. "DUTCH" RUPPERSBERGER, Maryland
ELEANOR HOLMES NORTON, District of Columbia
JIM COOPER, Tennessee
CHRIS BELL, Texas

BERNARD SANDERS, Vermont (Independent)

Peter Sirh, *Staff Director*
Melissa Wojciak, *Deputy Staff Director*
Randy Kaplan, *Senior Counsel/Parliamentarian*
Teresa Austin, *Chief Clerk*
Philip M. Schiliro, *Minority Staff Director*

CONTENTS

Page
Hearing held on April 4, 2003 1
Statement of:
Fauci, Dr. Anthony S., Director, National Institute of Allergy and Infectious Diseases, National Institutes of Health, Department of Health and Human Services; Dr. Mark McClellan, Commissioner, Food and Drug Administration, Department of Health and Human Services; Michael Brown, Under Secretary for Emergency Preparedness and Response, Department of Homeland Security; and Dr. Dale Klein, Assistant to the Secretary of Defense for Nuclear, Chemical and Biological Defense Programs, Department of Defense 15
Rapoport, Frank, attorney at law, McKenna Long & Aldridge, on behalf of Aventis Pasteur; Michael Friedman, chief medical officer for biomedical preparedness, Pharmaceutical Research and Manufacturers of America; Una Ryan, president, Avant Immunotherapeutics, Inc., Needham, MA; Katherine Bowdish, Ph.D., president, Alexion Antibody Technologies, Cheshire, CT; and John Edwards, chief of infectious diseases, Harbor-UCLA Medical Center, on behalf of the Infectious Diseases Society of America 65
Letters, statements, etc., submitted for the record by:
Brown, Michael, Under Secretary for Emergency Preparedness and Response, Department of Homeland Security, prepared statement of 39
Davis, Chairman Tom, a Representative in Congress from the State of Virginia, prepared statement of 3
Edwards, John, chief of infectious diseases, Harbor-UCLA Medical Center, on behalf of the Infectious Diseases Society of America, prepared statement of 105
Friedman, Michael, chief medical officer for biomedical preparedness, Pharmaceutical Research and Manufacturers of America, prepared statement of 77
Klein, Dale, Assistant to the Secretary of Defense for Nuclear, Chemical and Biological Defense Programs, Department of Defense, prepared statement of 45
McClellan, Dr. Mark, Commissioner, Food and Drug Administration, Department of Health and Human Services, prepared statement of 20
Rapoport, Frank, attorney at law, McKenna Long & Aldridge, on behalf of Aventis Pasteur, prepared statement of 68
Ryan, Una, president, Avant Immunotherapeutics, Inc., Needham, MA, prepared statement of 94
Shays, Hon. Christopher, a Representative in Congress from the State of Connecticut, prepared statement of 13
Waxman, Hon. Henry A., a Representative in Congress from the State of California, prepared statement of 7

PROJECT BIOSHIELD: CONTRACTING FOR THE HEALTH AND SECURITY OF THE AMERICAN PUBLIC

FRIDAY, APRIL 4, 2003

HOUSE OF REPRESENTATIVES,
COMMITTEE ON GOVERNMENT REFORM,
Washington, DC.

The committee met, pursuant to notice, at 9:30 a.m., in room 2154, Rayburn House Office Building, Hon. Tom Davis (chairman of the committee) presiding.

Present: Representatives Tom Davis, Shays, Waxman, Kucinich, Van Hollen and Norton.

Staff present: Peter Sirh, staff director; Melissa Wojciak, deputy staff director; Keith Ausbrook, chief counsel; Randy Kaplan, senior counsel; John Hunter and David Young, counsels; David Marin, director of communications; Scott Kopple, deputy director of communications; Teresa Austin, chief clerk; Joshua E. Gillespie, deputy clerk; Susie Schulte, legislative assistant; Corinne Zaccagnini, chief information officer; Phil Barnett, minority chief counsel; Karen Lightfoot, minority communications director/senior policy advisor; Mark Stephenson, minority professional staff member; Earley Green, minority chief clerk; Jean Gosa, minority assistant clerk; and Cecelia Morton, minority office manager.

Chairman TOM DAVIS. Good morning. A quorum being present, the Committee on Government Reform will come to order.

We are here today to examine an administration proposal known as the Project BioShield Act, which is designed to protect the health and safety of the American people in the event of a bioterrorist attack. This proposal, first announced by the President in his 2003 State of the Union address, authorizes the government to conduct and support the development, acquisition and distribution of vaccines, treatments and other biomedical countermeasures to use during public health emergencies, including bioterrorist attacks.

Over the past few decades, we have seen rapid progress in the development of treatments for many serious naturally occurring diseases. Pharmaceutical and biotechnology companies are highly capable of producing diagnostics and treatments to meet consumer demand. However, there has been little progress in treatments for deadly diseases like smallpox, anthrax, Ebola and plague, which currently affect few, if any, Americans. The reality is that for these diseases there is little manufacturer interest in developing necessary treatments, since there is no significant market other than the government.

Should the United States be attacked with these deadly pathogens, however, the need for vaccines, tests and treatments would be great; and it would be immediate. The administration's Project BioShield initiative is designed to ensure that the United States is prepared. The bill would stimulate companies to develop modern and effective vaccines, drugs and devices to protect Americans in the event of a bioterrorist attack or other public health emergency.

The bill has three main components: First, it sets up a process to expedite research and development of biomedical countermeasures. As part of this process, the Secretary of Health and Human Services would have flexible acquisition authorities to quickly and effectively buy cutting-edge products and services to support research, development, and production of vaccines and treatments. Additional acquisition flexibilities are put at the Secretary's disposal for the creation of a stockpile of these critical countermeasures. The Secretary would also have streamlined authority to hire technical experts and consultants.

Second, the Secretaries of Homeland Security and Health and Human Services would be required to work together to identify and evaluate bioterrorist threats and determine which countermeasures are needed to combat these threats. The bill would also create a permanent funding authority designed to spur the development of medicines and vaccines by the private sector.

Third, during national emergencies, the bill would permit the government to make available new and promising treatments prior to approval by the Food and Drug Administration.

A version of the Project BioShield Act is introduced by Senator Judd Gregg in the Senate and was reported out of the committee last month. I intend to introduce a House version in the near future.

We have assembled an impressive group of witnesses who will help us better understand this bill. I am particularly interested in learning how Project BioShield would assist in addressing the current public health emergency created by the epidemic known as Severe Acute Respiratory Syndrome [SARS]. More than 2,000 suspected cases of this mysterious disease have been reported in 17 nations, including the United States, with 78 fatalities. So far, there is no effective treatment or vaccine to combat this deadly syndrome.

I thank all of our witnesses for appearing today. I look forward to their testimony.

I would now yield to Mr. Waxman for his opening statement.

[The prepared statement of Chairman Tom Davis follows:]

Opening Statement
Chairman Tom Davis
Committee on Government Reform
"Project BioShield: Contracting for the Health and Security of the American Public"
April 4, 2003

We are here today to examine an Administration proposal, known as the Project Bioshield Act, which is designed to protect the health and safety of the American people in the event of a bioterrorist attack. This proposal, first announced by the President in his 2003 State of the Union Address, authorizes the government to conduct and support the development, acquisition, and distribution of vaccines, treatments, and other biomedical countermeasures to use during public health emergencies, including bioterrorist attacks.

Over the past few decades, we have seen rapid progress in the development of treatments for many serious naturally occurring diseases. Pharmaceutical and biotechnology companies are highly capable of producing diagnostics and treatments to meet consumer demand. However, there has been little progress in treatments for deadly diseases like smallpox, anthrax, Ebola, and plague, which affect few, if any Americans. The realty is that for these diseases, there is little manufacturer interest in developing necessary treatments, since there is no significant market, other than the government.

Should the United States be attacked with these deadly pathogens, however, the need for vaccines, tests, and treatments would be great and immediate. The Administration's Project Bioshield initiative is designed to ensure that the United States is prepared. The bill would stimulate companies to develop modern and effective vaccines, drugs, and devices to protect Americans in the event of a bioterrorist attack or other public health emergency.

The bill has three main components: First, it would set up a process to expedite research and development of biomedical countermeasures. As part of this process, the Secretary of Health and Human Services would have flexible acquisition authorities to quickly and effectively buy cutting edge products and services to support research, development, and production of vaccines and treatments. Additional acquisition flexibilities are put at the Secretary's disposal for the creation of a stockpile of these critical countermeasures. The Secretary would also have streamlined authority to hire technical experts and consultants.

Second, the Secretaries of Homeland Security and Health and Human Services would be required to work together to identify and evaluate bioterrorist threats and determine which countermeasures are needed to combat those threats. The bill would also create a permanent funding authority designed to spur the development of medicines and vaccines by the private sector.

Third, during national emergencies, the bill would permit the government to make available new and promising treatments prior to approval by the Food and Drug Administration.

A version of the Project Bioshield Act introduced by Senator Judd Gregg was reported out of Committee last month. I intend to introduce a House version in the near future.

We have assembled an impressive group of witnesses who will help us better understand this bill. I am particularly interested in learning how Project Bioshield would assist in addressing the current public health emergency created by the epidemic known as severe acute respiratory syndrome, or SARS. More than 2000 suspected cases of this mysterious disease have been reported in 17 nations, including the United States, with 78 fatalities. So far, there is no effective treatment or vaccine to combat this deadly syndrome.

###

Mr. WAXMAN. Thank you very much, Mr. Chairman.

I want to welcome the distinguished members of the panel, this first panel, and the subsequent panel as well.

We are holding a hearing on a proposal by the administration which I think all of us would support in its intent. We want to accomplish what the proposal would seek to have us accomplish, but our responsibility as Members of Congress is to scrutinize it carefully, to try to think about the unintended consequences, and to make sure that the job is done right.

The development of effective countermeasures to bioterrorism is certainly vital to our natural security. The Project BioShield represents a proposal to encourage the development of these products. We all support trying to do that, but we have a responsibility to look closely at the provisions of the legislation, and some of those provisions give me some cause for concern.

For example, the proposal removes important protections against waste and abuse that are standard for government contracts. I understand the concern that these protections, in an emergency situation, could impede the development of necessary products. However, any exceptions should be made only when necessary and should be subject to review. This proposal would make it nearly impossible for the courts, for Congress and even the executive branch to rein in abuses. The provision eliminating the government's access rights to contractors' books and records is particularly troubling.

Another provision permits products to be distributed without FDA approval. Here again, I recognize there may be unusual circumstances that would require this step in case of a dire emergency. However, the proposal's language is overly broad and could be used to support products that are simply not safe enough for FDA approval. This provision could also permit widespread distribution of unapproved drugs without informed consent, recordkeeping or reporting of adverse events.

The BioShield proposal also provides for unlimited guaranteed spending for procurement of vaccines and other countermeasures with little congressional guidance or limits on how much to spend.

This is a blank check approach. It could be looked at as an abdication of congressional responsibility. We should work to improve this proposal in such a way as to preserve oversight and recognize that, in order for BioShield to work, we need to assure that commitments made will be honored.

In this regard, it is ironic that the administration does not support a similar approach of assuring that commitments will be honored in the case of a smallpox vaccine compensation program. Here, the argument for mandatory spending is strong, because nurses, firefighters and other first responders deserve to know that they and their families will be supported in the case of severe injury or death. Yet in the case of smallpox vaccination compensation, the administration has proposed limiting compensation to the amount appropriated each year, explicitly refusing to guarantee its commitment to those Americans on the front lines of a bioterrorist attack. This inexplicable failure to assure funding is one of the reasons that the House voted down the administration's legislation on smallpox vaccines compensation last Monday.

I raised this issue last week in the Commerce Committee to point out the inconsistencies. At the time I did that, many people raised the point, why should we allow automatic spending in this area? They argued we shouldn't allow automatic spending in any area.

But Secretary Thompson made the case last week that we want to assure that funding will be there so that the companies that are taking the financial risk of developing these products know that they will be able to count on those funds.

I thought that was a strong argument to make. But, equally strong is to make the assurances clear that if a first responder gets immunized for smallpox that they are going to be able to count on funding should there be, in rare circumstances, but nevertheless in some circumstances, an adverse event.

Let me conclude by pointing out that the BioShield proposal includes provisions for public health emergencies, not just bioterrorism threats. The idea of including public health emergencies in a BioShield makes sense, because infectious diseases that occur in nature can claim many lives, can even become bioterrorist agents if intentionally spread.

What justifies government intervention to support countermeasures is that the market fails to encourage their development on its own. This rationale also applies to the development of treatments for potential public health emergencies.

In 2002, not a single new antimicrobial drug was approved by FDA; and apparently only a handful are in development by major pharmaceutical companies. One reason may be that the market for the few cases of multidrug-resistant bacteria is currently quite small. That leads to a market failure. And yet the need for such treatments is enormous.

Just yesterday, the New England Journal of Medicine carried the first report of a common bacteria that is extremely resistant to an antibiotic that is usually the last line of defense.

If properly designed, then, BioShield can serve valuable purposes, improving our preparedness against bioterrorist attacks and natural epidemics.

I look forward to hearing from the witnesses today to help us understand this proposal and find ways to improve it. We need to work together collaboratively for what is certainly a shared goal that we all have.

Thank you.

Chairman TOM DAVIS. Thank you very much.

[The prepared statement of Hon. Henry A. Waxman follows:]

Statement of Rep. Henry A. Waxman
Project BioShield:
Contracting for the Health and Security of the American Public
April 4, 2003

Given the serious threat of bioterrorism, the development of effective countermeasures is vital to our national security. Project BioShield represents the Administration's proposal to encourage the development of these products. I fully support the intent of this legislation. I also agree with its premise -- that when the market cannot foster the development of critical products by itself, the government must rise to the challenge.

Nonetheless, the importance of the mission must not obscure the need to do it right.

We have a responsibility to look closely at the provisions of this legislation. And some of the provisions give me cause for concern.

For example, the proposal removes important protections against waste and abuse that are standard for government contracts. I understand the concern that these protections, in emergency situations, could impede the development of necessary products. However, any exceptions should be made only when necessary and should be subject to review. This proposal would make it nearly impossible for courts, Congress, and even the executive branch to rein in abuses. The provision eliminating the government's access rights to contractors' books and records is particularly troubling.

Another provision permits products to be distributed without FDA approval. Here again, I recognize that there may be unusual circumstances that would require this step in case of a dire emergency. However, the proposal's language is overly broad and could be used to support products that simply are not safe enough for FDA approval. The provision could also permit widespread distribution of unapproved drugs without informed consent, recordkeeping, or reporting of adverse events.

The BioShield proposal also provides for unlimited guaranteed spending for the procurement of vaccines and other countermeasures, with little congressional guidance or limits on how much to spend.

This blank check approach is an abdication of congressional responsibility. We should work to improve this proposal in such a way as to preserve oversight, and recognize that, in order for BioShield to work, we need to assure that commitments made will be honored.

In this regard, it is ironic that the Administration does not support a similar approach of assuring that commitments will be honored in the case of a smallpox vaccine compensation program. Here, the argument for mandatory spending is strong, because nurses, firefighters and other first responders deserve to know that they and their families will be supported in the event of severe injury or death. Yet in the case of smallpox compensation, the Administration has proposed limiting compensation to the amount appropriated each year, explicitly refusing to guarantee its commitment to those Americans on the front lines of a bioterrorist attack. This inexplicable failure to assure funding is one of the reasons that the House voted down the Administration's legislation on Monday.

Let me conclude by pointing out that the BioShield proposal includes provisions for public health emergencies, not just bioterrorism threats. The idea of including public health emergencies in a BioShield makes sense, because infectious diseases that occur in nature can claim many lives and can even become bioterrorist agents if intentionally spread.

What justifies government intervention to support countermeasures is that the market fails to encourage their development on its own. This rationale also applies to the development of treatments for potential public health emergencies. In 2002, not a single new antimicrobial drug was approved by FDA, and apparently only a handful are in development by major pharmaceutical companies. One reason may be that the market for the few cases of multidrug resistant bacteria is currently quite small.

Yet the need for such treatments is enormous.

Just yesterday, the *New England Journal of Medicine* carried the first report of a common bacteria that is extremely resistant to an antibiotic that is usually the last line of defense.

If properly designed, then, BioShield can serve valuable purposes, improving our preparedness against both bioterrist attacks and natural epidemics.

I look forward to hearing from the witnesses today to help us understand this proposal and find ways to improve it.

Chairman TOM DAVIS. The gentleman from Connecticut, the vice chairman of the committee, is recognized. Mr. Shays.

Mr. SHAYS. Thank you, Mr. Chairman, for convening this very important hearing.

I come to this discussion with significant skepticism, not about the urgency of the problem of countering biological threats but about the adequacy and efficacy of the proposed solution.

Buying biologics is not like buying bullets. The cold war model of short-term research incentives and artificial markets to sustain defense contractors may not fit the intensely entrepreneurial pharmaceutical and biomedical industries. The Department of Defense [DOD], Joint Vaccine Acquisition Program and the Anthrax Vaccine Immunization Program should serve as cautionary tales. The latter rushed to procure last century technology to the detriment of research and development of a modern anthrax vaccine. The former spent 6 years and more than $300 million but has yet to finish a single vaccine.

As the current outbreak of Severe Acute Respiratory Syndrome [SARS] attests, we remain hard-pressed to maintain our defenses against nature's evolving arsenal of biological threats. Hasty acquisition of medical countermeasures available within 5 years, as proposed in BioShield, applies only a short-term bandage to a long-term illness.

Massive caches of stockpiled vaccines, antibiotics and drugs will protect no one if they cannot be administered quickly and safely. The missing element of the protective shield envisioned in this proposal is public health capacity.

Surveillance systems, diagnostic tools and trained medical personnel are prerequisites to any effective defense against natural and man-made biological outbreaks.

I look forward, Mr. Chairman, to discussing the BioShield proposal and biopreparedness priorities with our witnesses this morning. This is truly a very important hearing and one to which we should pay close attention.

Chairman TOM DAVIS. Thank you very much.

[The prepared statement of Hon. Christopher Shays follows:]

ONE HUNDRED EIGHTH CONGRESS

Congress of the United States

House of Representatives

COMMITTEE ON GOVERNMENT REFORM

2157 RAYBURN HOUSE OFFICE BUILDING
WASHINGTON, DC 20515–6143

MAJORITY (202) 225–5074
FACSIMILE (202) 225–3974
MINORITY (202) 225–5051
TTY (202) 225–6852

www.house.gov/reform

SUBCOMMITTEE ON NATIONAL SECURITY, EMERGING THREATS,
AND INTERNATIONAL RELATIONS

Christopher Shays, Connecticut
Chairman
Room B-372 Rayburn Building
Washington, D.C. 20515
Tel: 202 225-2546
Fax: 202 225-2382
E-mail: hr.groc@mail.house gov

Statement of Rep. Christopher Shays
April 4, 2003

Thank you, Mr. Chairman.

I come to this discussion with significant skepticism, not about the urgency of the problem of countering biological threats, but about the adequacy and efficacy of the proposed solution.

Buying biologics is not like buying bullets. The Cold War model of short-term research incentives and artificial markets that sustained defense contractors may not fit the intensely entrepreneurial pharmaceutical and biomedical industries. The Department of Defense (DOD) Joint Vaccine Acquisition Program and the Anthrax Vaccine Immunization Program should serve as cautionary tales. The latter rushed to procure last century technology to the detriment of research and development of a modern anthrax vaccine. The former spent six years and more than $300 million, but has yet to finish a single vaccine.

As the current outbreak of Severe Acute Respiratory Syndrome (SARS) attests, we remain hard-pressed to maintain our defenses against nature's evolving arsenal of biological threats. Hasty acquisition of medical countermeasures available within five years, as proposed in BioShield, applies only a short-term bandage to a long-term illness.

Massive caches of stockpiled vaccines, antibiotics and drugs will protect no one if they cannot be administered quickly and safely. The missing element of the protective shield envisioned in this proposal is public health capacity. Surveillance systems, diagnostic tools and trained medical personnel are prerequisites to any effective defense against natural and manmade biological outbreaks.

I look forward to discussing the BioShield proposal and bio-preparedness priorities with our witnesses this morning.

Chairman TOM DAVIS. We now move to our first panel of witnesses. I want to thank our witnesses for appearing today.

We have Dr. Anthony Fauci from the National Institute of Allergy and Infectious Diseases; Dr. Mark McClellan, the Commissioner of the Food and Drug Administration; from the Department of Homeland Security, we have Michael Brown, who is the Under Secretary for Emergency Preparedness and Response; and rounding out the first panel is Dr. Dale Klein, who is the Assistant to the Secretary of Defense for Nuclear, Chemical and Biological Defense Programs.

It is the policy of this committee that witnesses be sworn. So if you would stand with me and raise your right hands.

[Witnesses sworn.]

Chairman TOM DAVIS. Dr. Fauci, we will start with you and move right down the line. Thank you for being with us.

STATEMENTS OF DR. ANTHONY S. FAUCI, DIRECTOR, NATIONAL INSTITUTE OF ALLERGY AND INFECTIOUS DISEASES, NATIONAL INSTITUTES OF HEALTH, DEPARTMENT OF HEALTH AND HUMAN SERVICES; DR. MARK McCLELLAN, COMMISSIONER, FOOD AND DRUG ADMINISTRATION, DEPARTMENT OF HEALTH AND HUMAN SERVICES; MICHAEL BROWN, UNDER SECRETARY FOR EMERGENCY PREPAREDNESS AND RESPONSE, DEPARTMENT OF HOMELAND SECURITY; AND DR. DALE KLEIN, ASSISTANT TO THE SECRETARY OF DEFENSE FOR NUCLEAR, CHEMICAL AND BIOLOGICAL DEFENSE PROGRAMS, DEPARTMENT OF DEFENSE

Dr. FAUCI. I appreciate the opportunity to discuss Project BioShield with you today.

As you know from the legislative language, the purpose of Project BioShield is to accelerate the research, development and purchase and availability of effective medical countermeasures against chemical, biological, radiological and nuclear terrorism and public health emergencies.

Project BioShield, as you, Mr. Chairman, summarized so well, is a three-pronged program. It increases the authorities of and flexibilities of the NIH to expedite research, it establishes a secure funding source to purchase countermeasures, and it establishes an FDA emergency use authorization.

I am going to very briefly discuss the first two components in the context of how they relate to the work at the NIH; and my HHS colleague, Dr. Mark McClellan, the FDA Commissioner, will discuss both the procurement issues and how they relate in the context of the FDA's responsibilities.

The NIH research system has served the country and the world extraordinarily well for many decades. The NIH employs traditional funding mechanisms that include grants, contracts, cooperative agreements and other partnerships as well as time-tested personnel functions, a system that has resulted in numerous major advances that have improved the health of the Nation, including the development of interventions for a number of emerging and reemerging infectious diseases.

However, the events of September 11, 2001, and the subsequent anthrax attacks have changed, probably forever, how the biomedical community is going to respond to emerging threats. We are now in a wartime mode and are compelled to modify the way that we do business without compromising the elements that have made us so successful.

With regard to the first component of Project BioShield, the legislation provides for a number of special authorities at NIH that will have the aggregate effect of expediting the research process. This is what we call the push toward the countermeasure development. Among those, BioShield provides for expedited peer review of grants and contracts, and I emphasize without compromising the scientific, technical and programmatic standards. It also streamlines procurement authority, bolsters authorities for acquisition and renovation of facilities, expedites personal services contracts and provides flexibility with regard to personnel authority. We feel that these expanded authorities will considerably hasten the pathway from basic research concept up to and including effective countermeasure development.

Let me switch gears quickly and speak briefly about the mandated appropriations authority for the procurement of countermeasures. We at NIH and our colleagues at DHHS have had numerous occasions to discuss the development of countermeasures with companies ranging from small biotech firms to big PLRMA. These are our industrial partners that are essential to bringing countermeasure development to fruition.

Many of those firms are willing to help in the development of biodefense countermeasures, but the fact remains that they are business and are not nonprofit organizations, and they need a tangible incentive to get involved.

Now when it is evident that a given product has a potential to make a profit, few incentives are needed to engage industry. However, when you are dealing with a product for which there is no guarantee of a return or for which the market is tenuous, these companies clearly need some assurances that there will ultimately be a return for their investment. Without such assurances, they will simply pursue the development of other products.

When we meet with companies, we hear one of two things. First, they may already be involved in the early stages of development of biodefense countermeasures on their own initiative. They are willing to take on a fair amount of risk, but they want some assurances if they are actually successful that there will be a market for their product. Many state, quite frankly, that they do not want to be vulnerable to the vicissitudes of the cyclical appropriation process, as sound as that is in so many arenas.

The other scenario in which we are trying to engage reluctant companies to get involved, namely people who have many other things to do with their efforts and with their expertise, in this instance, we do as we are doing now. We push with discretionary research dollars.

However, in our experience, that does not seem to be enough. With Project BioShield, we will further be able to tell these companies that they can partner with us such that if at their end they meet milestones and come up with a licensable countermeasure they have our assurances that there will be money available to them for advanced procurement and, ultimately, purchase.

These are examples of what we call the pull of the process.

In summary, the accelerated development of effective countermeasures against terrorism requires a new research paradigm and new ways to engage our industrial partners. Project BioShield will help us meet the challenges of bioterrorism effectively and expeditiously.

Thank you again, Mr. Chairman and members of the committee, for the opportunity to testify today about this important initiative to improve our homeland security; and I would be happy to take questions after the others.

Chairman TOM DAVIS. Thank you, Dr. Fauci.

Dr. McClellan.

Dr. MCCLELLAN. Mr. Chairman, Congressman Waxman, distinguished members and staff of the committee, thank you for inviting me here today to discuss the Project BioShield Act of 2003.

As you know, FDA has been engaged with other government agencies and the private sector in an accelerated major new focus on helping to develop and make available better countermeasures for biological, chemical, radiological attacks and other types of attacks. This bill will significantly enhance those efforts and improve our ability to protect our citizens from these threats. In light of the heightened security risk facing our Nation and our troops, we appreciate your timely consideration of finding better ways to acquire the countermeasures that we need.

I am pleased to tell you that in the last 2 months alone we have approved safe and effective treatments for certain nerve gases and radiological agents. We have enhanced our stockpiles of vaccines and treatments for smallpox and other possible agents of biowarfare.

Working with the Department of Health and Human Services, particularly NIH, as well as DOD and the Department of Homeland Security and private companies, we are taking further steps to determine as quickly as possible whether other available agents may be of benefit. Such products include drugs that may be active against smallpox and viral hemorrhagic fever, new treatments for exposure to radiologic agents, as well as novel treatments for smallpox and anthrax vaccines and immunoglobulins to treat botulism or complications of smallpox vaccinations. We are also working on some new diagnostic and treatment methods for the Severe Acute Respiratory Syndrome.

FDA recognizes that early and ongoing consultation with product developers is essential to get rapid approval of safe and executive products.

We focused intense efforts on the rapid turnaround of requests for information, review of study plans and data, development of plans for appropriate product production and use where needed under streamlined investigational new drug procedures for agents of terror, for treating agents of terrorism.

Our experience with the approval of a new treatment for the effects of a certain nerve gas, pyridostigmine, was approved under a new animal rule as a result of legislation last year. In this case, FDA worked closely with the sponsors of the application to define not only the criteria that would help in evaluating the drug's safety and effectiveness for this use, we also worked closely to develop appropriate animal models that ultimately helped us verify safety and efficacy.

At the same time, we realize that we can't easily solve the problem of getting safe and effective countermeasures to the public with the existing financial incentives for developing them. Our close work with the developers of these new products, which now includes around 200 professional staff in our biologic program alone, has reminded us that proof of concept is still a very long way from large-scale production of effective countermeasures that pose acceptable safety risks.

In some cases, we have done the work to demonstrate safety and effectiveness of certain products for counterterrorism use, but we don't yet have companies willing to produce these products. To bring badly needed, safer and more effective countermeasures to our Nation's defense, we are going to need to do more to encourage all parties, basic science researchers and government labs as well as the major medical companies, to take up the cause of developing countermeasures.

Consequently, while the countermeasures we have made available already have given us a deeper and more effective stockpile of treatments, in many cases they are based on old technologies. For example, monoclonal antibodies have changed the way that we treat everything from heart disease to cancer. It is considered a master technology in many biomedical circles.

Many researchers believe that this technology can be effectively applied to developing countermeasures from anthrax and botulinum toxins to even the Ebola virus. Yet there is only limited research at the developmental stage into the application of these bioterrorism countermeasures. Instead, there is currently available an antitoxin to botulism, which is based on a technology that was available when the FDA came into existence in 1906. This is a useful and very-much-needed treatment, but there is strong reason to believe that new technology can produce antidotes and vaccines that are even safer and more effective and so much more valuable, and that is what has been available to us now.

So I agree with Congressman Shays about the need to get to a next generation of countermeasures through this approach.

Research and development into next generations countermeasures has been much slower for naturally occurring diseases, largely because there is no clear financial reward for success. Many companies that I have talked to, just like Tony has, know that the development of medical products is a very uncertain process. They are used to taking risks and knowing that they might fail, but what they want to know is that if they succeed there is a certainty of a reasonable financial reward.

Today, when it comes to countermeasures, there are plenty of risks but few clear defined rewards; and that is why Project BioShield is critically important. It includes new procurement authorities to provide certainty of payment in advance for the delivery of effective new products. By creating conditions for a market that is reasonable, predictable and consistent over time, government will set the stage for the private sector to make the investments and problem-solving efforts required to develop more effective next-generation countermeasures.

Furthermore, in the event that a national emergency has been declared, the bill allows for a limited and highly targeted use of countermeasures for treating a select agent without the completion of the full FDA process. To be clear, this would only occur if a product in the approval pipeline is urgently needed because there are no effective approved treatments available and if we conclude that in the emergency the product's potential benefits outweigh its potential risks for those persons who don't have a better alternative.

We expect more antidotes and vaccines to flow out of BioShield, and at FDA we are ready to help facilitate their development and to make sure the best available treatment can be used effectively in an emergency. We live in a new biomedical era today. It is an era of great promise but also of very serious risks in the years ahead from those who would deliberately use biological, chemical, radiologic and other agents as weapons of mass destruction.

In addition to the great need for translating biomedical research breakthroughs into effective new treatments for naturally occurring diseases like cancer and Alzheimers and antibiotic resistant bacterial infections, we also need to create much-needed new incentives and authorities to respond to these unnatural threats.

We are proud to be able to participate in this process to help the Nation, and we appreciate the strong bipartisan effort in both the House and the Senate to respond to this urgent critical challenge.

Thank you, and after the panel's introductory statements, I will be glad to take questions as well.

Chairman TOM DAVIS. Thank you very much.

[The prepared statement of Mr. McClellan follows:]

Statement of

Dr. Mark B. McClellan, Commissioner, Food and Drug Administration
and
Dr. Anthony S. Fauci, Director, National Institute of Allergy and Infectious Diseases, National Institutes of Health

Before the
House Government Reform Committee

"PROJECT BIOSHIELD"

For Release on Delivery
Friday, April 4, 2003

Chairman Davis, Congressman Waxman, and Members of the Committee, thank you for holding this hearing today to discuss the Administration bill, the Project BioShield Act of 2003. As you know, the Department of Health and Human Services has been heavily engaged in the Federal government's efforts to prevent, prepare for, and respond to acts of terrorism, particularly those involving chemical, biological, radiological and nuclear threat agents. This bill is a continuation of such efforts. It would enable the Government to develop, procure, and make available countermeasures to chemical, biological, radiological, and nuclear agents for use in a public health emergency that affects national security.

Although only the procurement and personnel provisions of this proposed legislation fall under the jurisdiction of the Government Reform Committee, Project BioShield is best understood when viewed in its entirety. It is important to appreciate how each of the three components contained in this proposal interact to quickly and safely develop and make available lifesaving bioterrorism countermeasures. As such, we would like to take this opportunity to describe the three main components of Project BioShield.

Pharmaceutical research and development historically has focused on development of products likely to attract significant commercial interest. Many countermeasures for potential agents of terrorism realistically have no market other than the government and thus have not generated a great deal of manufacturer interest. Because the market for developing medical countermeasures against terrorism is speculative private companies have not invested and engaged in developing the medical countermeasures that the current situation warrants. However, in the vaccine development area, representatives of the pharmaceutical industry have stressed that, to the extent that the federal government can define its vaccine requirements and assure up front that the requisite funds will be available to purchase the vaccines, the industry will meet the challenge.

In these post-9/11 times of increased potential for chemical, biological, radiological, and nuclear and other terrorist attacks, it is important now more than ever for the United States to take all necessary steps to protect its citizens from these agents. The current security environment dictates the need for rapid acquisition of countermeasures. Armed with technology that only recently was the stuff of science fiction, the U. S. armed forces are better equipped than ever to take military actions against threats to our national security and defend U.S. citizens against missiles, aircraft, guns and other traditional weaponry. But other not-so-traditional threats are lurking. Our enemies seek, and in some cases have already obtained, biological, chemical, radiological and nuclear weapons that could penetrate our military defenses and civilian surveillance systems, and cause significant harm. We need your help to confront these threats to our homeland.

The possibility of the intentional use of chemical, biological, radiological, and nuclear agents presents a true threat to our society. You have heard about many of these threats: anthrax, smallpox, tularemia, botulinum toxin, hemorrhagic fevers and plague. We will fight these new weapons, not with bombs and guns, but with countermeasures such as vaccines, therapeutics, and early diagnosis. We may be called upon to provide mass inoculation or drug treatment. The personnel who will lead the efforts to develop, acquire, regulate, and administer these medical tools will not necessarily wear military uniforms or be headquartered at the Pentagon. They are civilian administrators and scientists of the Department of Health and Human Services located in such places as the Centers for Disease Control and Prevention (CDC), the Food and Drug Administration (FDA) and the National Institutes of Health (NIH), as well as State and local health officials.

We are making rapid progress in acquiring countermeasures for the agents of greatest concern such as smallpox, anthrax, and botulism toxin and have made advances in development of new products. We have sufficient Aventis smallpox vaccine to vaccinate the country in an emergency and the new ACAM2000 cell culture vaccine is coming into the stockpile at a rapid rate. We expect to have 155 million doses by this summer. NIH initiated the industrial development of a safer next generation smallpox vaccine by signing two contracts with manufacturers last month. On the NIH campus, a new, potentially safer smallpox vaccine entered the first stage of human testing. We currently have a stockpile of antibiotics to deal with an attack with anthrax, plague and tularemia. In addition, we have access to a stockpile of the current anthrax vaccine and are optimistic that an accelerated development program involving two manufacturers begun last October will result in production of a new recombinant anthrax vaccine sometime next year partially with BioShield funding. Tularemia and plague vaccines are in the research phase and expected to move into advanced development within 2 years. We also have acquired additional quantities of botulinum antoxins for the treatment of botulism.

Because of a relative lack of focused research on terrorist agents, the medical treatments available for some types of terrorist attacks have improved little in decades while there has been tremendous and rapid progress in the treatment of serious natural-occurring diseases. At a time when Americans must confront the realities of terrorism directed at the United States, it is imperative that the Federal government be prepared to protect our citizens from potential agents of bioterrorism.

Many of the available countermeasures have been made using traditional, older technologies, and some have significant side effects (e.g., the traditional "Dryvax" smallpox vaccine). Newer products produced using advanced technologies such as the production of recombinant anthrax or botulinum toxin proteins or more attenuated viral strains to protect against smallpox hold out hope of reducing adverse reactions while maintaining effective protection. Extensive studies must be performed to assure that these products are both safe and effective. Showing effectiveness when diseases do not occur naturally can be challenging and requires the use of appropriate animal models and careful studies of the critical immune responses to a vaccine. These studies are best planned with close interaction between government scientists and the countermeasure sponsors. Such early product development planning has been going on in partnership with FDA, NIH, CDC, and others (e.g. the development and evaluation of new smallpox and anthrax vaccines). Other examples where older vaccines or other technologies have been employed (often effectively) include vaccines for plague and anthrax and immunoglobulins for treating smallpox vaccine complications and botulism. Also, the promise of rapid productions of large amounts of monoclonal antibodies that could be used to protect against a variety of bioterrorist pathogens or vaccine adverse events is becoming a reality.

This must be a public and private partnership. The pathway from idea to final product is complex. The optimal scientific approach to identifying the best drug and vaccine candidates must be based on laboratory studies. Testing must be performed in appropriate animal models to document safety and appropriate protective or treatment response, and to help determine dosing. Human studies must be carefully initiated to assure the basic safety of the product, and then appropriate dosing and response must be determined based on measurements of levels of drug or antibody predicted to have a protective effect. Steps must be taken to assure that the materials used to make the countermeasures ---and the final product itself--- can be manufactured safely, free of contaminants, and with reproducible and predictable purity, potency, and composition. Careful trials in humans, or where not possible, animal models, must be performed to show that the product is safe and effective for the types of populations which might receive it and against the methods of infection or exposure that could be encountered. All of these steps require careful planning, experience, and ongoing management and scientific evaluation. Costs to develop and manufacture high quality biological products and perform and evaluate the needed animal and human studies are high. Grants and contract mechanisms may not always be sufficient or attract the most experienced manufacturers. Manufacturing capacity for biological products, particularly for vaccines, is not substantial. For all these reasons, the best possible support and public-private partnerships and teamwork are essential.

The President announced BioShield in his 2003 State of the Union Address. This is a key legislative priority for this Administration. The BioShield bill is designed to speed the development and availability of medical countermeasures in response to the current threats our Nation faces. The goals of Project BioShield are: 1) to accelerate and streamline government research on countermeasures; 2) to create incentives for private companies to develop countermeasures for inclusion in the stockpile; and, 3) to give the government the ability to make these products widely available quickly in a public health emergency in order to protect our citizens from an attack using a select agent. This legislation is a critical component of our Nation's homeland security strategy.

The three major provisions of the Bill are described below.

Expediting Research and Development at NIH

First, the Department, working primarily through the National Institute of Allergy and Infectious Diseases at NIH, would be given new authorities to speed research and development in promising areas of medical countermeasures against potential bioterrorism agents. The increased authority will provide additional flexibility in awarding contracts, cooperative agreements, and grants for research and development of medical countermeasures including vaccines, drugs, biologics, and diagnostics, and streamlined authority to hire necessary technical experts. Funding awards would remain subject to rigorous scientific peer review, but expedited peer review procedures could be used when appropriate.

NIH is leading the Federal government's campaign to improve the Nation's public health through biomedical research. The major reason that NIH has been entrusted with this vital leadership role is its proven record in combating naturally occurring emerging and re-emerging diseases, which is fortified by its rigorous system for ensuring that only the best science is supported by Federal dollars. Underpinning NIH's research is a rigorous peer review system, which brings together top experts from the public and private sectors of scientific research, as well as patient representatives and other members of the public, to evaluate research grant applications. NIH applies stringent management controls over contracts, personnel, leasing, and construction to ensure careful and responsible use of taxpayer dollars. These safeguards have served the country well. Currently, NIH is leading us through the greatest era of discovery in the history of medical research.

The President's Project BioShield initiative is intended to speed up NIH research and advanced development in targeted areas by providing more flexible authorities for NIH including procurement and personnel recruitment for critical biodefense work. Our BioShield proposal would authorize the Secretary of Health and Human Services, acting through NIH, to simplify and expedite acquisition requirements for material and services through such mechanisms as raising the dollar threshold for simplified acquisitions and using noncompetitive procedures when necessary. The Act would allow the Secretary to expedite scientific peer review requirements in urgent circumstances, but still require a process of quality review.

Project BioShield is intended to strike a balance, during times of crisis, between the Federal government's need to guarantee that the best research is conducted effectively and efficiently, and the national need to have a quick turnaround in responding to biological, chemical, and nuclear weapons of terror. With the authorities contained in the Act, we can improve our ability to respond to chemical, biological, radiological or nuclear attacks against American citizens and soldiers.

It often takes many months to issue research grants, engage pharmaceutical companies to manufacture vaccines and other drug therapies, hire personnel and consultants, or acquire material and services. In times of emergency, we cannot afford the time that it currently takes to accomplish these goals and events. We need vaccines and drugs to fight bioweapons right now. We need expertise right now. We need to build biocontainment facilities to conduct research right now. Project BioShield gives us the tools to cut through red tape and accomplish our mission.

Procurement of Countermeasures

Second, and perhaps most important to this Committee, as it falls under your jurisdiction, the Administration's bill creates a new permanent, indefinite funding authority within the

Department of Homeland Security (DHS) to procure medical countermeasures for inclusion in the DHS Strategic National Stockpile. This Department will play a major role along with DHS in identifying and evaluating critical biomedical countermeasures. Certain countermeasures, including antibiotics, are procured and distributed by the Department of Veterans Affairs' National Acquisition System. A great deal of work has been done to identify vaccines and antitoxins that would be needed to protect the U.S. population from dangerous pathogens, e.g. anthrax, smallpox, botulinum toxin, tularemia, Ebola, and plague. In the interest of national security and public health, it is essential that the Administration engage in the process as early as possible with sponsors and organizations that are developing the therapeutics, vaccines, and other countermeasures. This Department will maintain a proactive role to help ensure that the products are developed as efficiently as possible.

The Administration already has identified several products as promising countermeasures and is meeting with sponsors to help foster the successful development of these products. Such products include new generation smallpox and anthrax vaccines and therapies to treat botulism, plague, and Ebola and other hemorrhagic diseases.

The bill requires the HHS and DHS Secretaries to identify specific countermeasures that would be appropriate for procurement and, in coordination with the OMB Director, make recommendations to the President. The following determinations must be made in order for the DHS and HHS Secretaries to make a procurement recommendation: 1. determination of material threats, including risk of use and the public health impact; 2. an assessment of the availability and appropriateness of certain countermeasures to address the specific threats identified in the first determination; and 3. determination of countermeasures that are appropriate for procurement under BioShield. This third determination includes: (a) determination that the product is a qualified countermeasure (the bill defines a qualified countermeasure as a drug or biologic product that is approved or licensed by FDA or one that is likely to be FDA approved or licensed within five years); (b). determination of quantities needed and feasibility of production and distribution; and (c). determination of no significant commercial market for the product other than as a homeland security threat countermeasure. This authority will enable the government to purchase vaccines and therapies for which no other significant commercial market exists, as soon as experts believe that the countermeasures can be made safe and effective.

The Administration has carefully constructed this system of technical determinations and processes leading to a recommendation to the President because of the extraordinary nature of the proposal for permanent, indefinite funding authority. The Administration is committed to ensuring that recommendations to use this new authority are carefully considered with input from all experts within the Executive Branch, and that the final determination to exercise this spending authority is made by the President. Any countermeasures that do not meet the criteria laid out in our bill, or that are otherwise determined not to be appropriate for procurement through this authority, may still be purchased through the existing DHS discretionary stockpile authority.

The Administration recognizes that no other significant commercial market exists for many of these products that will be needed to protect our military and civilian population. This authority will enable the government to purchase vaccines, therapies and other interventions provided experts believe that the countermeasures can be made safe and effective. The Secretary of HHS and the Secretary of DHS will collaborate in identifying these critical medical countermeasures, by evaluating likely threats, new opportunities in biomedical research and development, and other public health considerations.

Emergency Use Authorization

The FDA approval process for drugs, devices, and biological products is the gold standard for the world. Sixty percent of the world's drugs are introduced first in the United States. Research and development pipelines hold the promise of dramatically advanced treatments, thanks to breakthroughs in genomics, proteomics, nanotechnologies, and other biomedical sciences. In the years ahead, we can look forward to more sophisticated, individualized, and effective treatments. Our policies and regulations help ensure that products that get to market are safe and effective. In addition to animal studies, sponsors of new drugs and vaccines typically conduct three phases of clinical trials in humans to demonstrate the safety and efficacy of a product. This process can take years, and is procedurally cumbersome.

In preparing for the challenges we face today, we may not always have a desirable amount of time to address the threat presented by agents of bioterrorism. The current FDA approval process is too long to be used during emergency situations. We have some mechanisms in place to get products to market faster, e.g. the accelerated approval mechanism, and expedited review. The animal efficacy rule provides a new avenue for approval for products whose efficacy cannot be tested in human clinical trials. The single patient IND process and the treatment IND process permit access to unapproved products. However, these mechanisms alone are not sufficient in an emergency.

This Bill will permit the Government to make new and promising treatments still under development available quickly, if needed, for use in emergency situations where no effective approved or licensed products are available, potentially saving many lives. This authorization will only be used when a national emergency has been declared. In the absence of FDA approval of a product for a specific countermeasure use, the BioShield Bill permits the HHS Secretary to issue an emergency authorization that would provide Americans with access to certain unlicensed countermeasures. The Secretary has discretion to facilitate the availability of these important products. Before issuing an emergency authorization, the HHS Secretary must make the following conclusions:

- the agent specified in the determination can cause serious or life-threatening disease;
- the product may reasonably be believed to be effective in detecting, diagnosing, treating, or preventing the disease;
- the benefits of the product may reasonably be believed to outweigh its risks;

- there is no adequate alternative to the product that is approved and available; and
- any other criteria prescribed in regulation are met.

This bill would allow use of the best technology available at the time of a declared emergency. The emergency use authorization would remain in effect no more than one year, unless the specific terrorist threat justifies extension of the authorization.

FDA regulations are stringent when it comes to informed consent for investigational products. Because urgent situations may require mass inoculations and/or drug treatments, such informed consent requirements may prove impossible to implement within the necessary time frame when trying to achieve the public health goal of protecting Americans from the imminent danger. The legislation would provide for the Secretary to impose conditions on the authorization, either by regulation or on a case-by-case basis, where appropriate to protect public health. Specifically, the bill provides that such conditions shall include labeling and other requirements to ensure that health care professionals are informed of the special emergency nature of the authorization; of the benefits and risks (and the extent to which such benefits and risks are unknown); and of the alternatives to the product, and their benefits and risks. In addition, the conditions of authorization may include the following:

- labeling and other requirements to ensure that patients are informed of the special emergency nature of the authorization; of the benefits and risks (and the extent to which such benefits and risks are unknown); of any option to refuse the product; and of the alternatives to the product, and their benefits and risks;

- limitations on who may distribute the product and how distribution should be performed;
- limitations on who may administer the product, to whom it may be administered, and when it may be administered;
- requirements to perform further studies or clinical trials;
- record keeping and reporting requirements;
- requirements, or waiver of otherwise-applicable requirements, regarding good manufacturing practice; and
- requirements for monitoring and reporting adverse events.

The language of this bill is narrowly tailored to address the essential components for use of an emergency authorization. It provides specific conditions and criteria for issuance of such an authorization. It requires a declaration of emergency and provides for a limited duration of use. It gives the Secretary authority to require record keeping and access to records. Finally, it provides civil monetary penalties for violations.

Conclusion

The Department of Health and Human Services is committed to ensuring the health and medical care of our citizens. Project BioShield is another step towards enhancing our Nation's ability to respond to biological or chemical threats.

In summary, our BioShield proposal would:

- Ensure that sufficient resources are available to procure the next generation of countermeasures;
- Accelerate NIH research and development by providing more flexibility in the contracting process, procurement authorities, and grant making for critical biodefense work; and,
- Make promising treatments available more quickly for use in emergencies by establishing new emergency use authorization procedures at the FDA.

Mr. Chairman and members of the Committee, we seek your bipartisan support to move this issue forward and support this bill. We look forward to working closely with this and other Committees to pass this important legislation and improve our nation's preparedness for and response capability to the threat of bioterrorism.

Chairman TOM DAVIS. Mr. Brown.

Mr. BROWN. Thank you, Mr. Chairman, Mr. Shays and Mr. Waxman.

My name is Michael Brown. I am the Under Secretary for Emergency Preparedness and Response Directorate of the Department of Homeland Security. I am honored to appear before you today on behalf of Secretary Ridge to discuss our role in bioterrorism preparedness in general, and in BioShield specifically. Preparing our citizens for the event of a bioterrorism event is one of several significant challenges that the new Department faces.

But before I discuss the Emergency Preparedness and Response's role in BioShield, I want to give you a broader perspective about our mission.

Members of Congress have been very good to us in our years as an independent agency, the Federal Emergency Management Agency. But we are pleased to join the Department of Homeland Security and bring a wealth of knowledge from our experiences in preparing for, mitigating against, responding to, and recovering from disasters of all kinds.

I want to assure the members of this committee that EP&R will not lose sight of its responsibility of helping people and communities affected by disaster. The mission statement of the Directorate—to lead the Nation to prepare for, mitigate the effects of, respond to and recover from major domestic disasters, both natural and man-made, including acts of terrorism—contains the same core responsibilities that guided the Federal Emergency Management Agency.

During fiscal year 2002, FEMA expended nearly $3.9 billion in disaster funds to aid people and communities who were overwhelmed by disasters, which included earthquakes, floods and ice and winter storms, fires, hurricanes, tornados and tropical storms. FEMA has responded to 42 major disasters, including 37 States and 4 of the U.S. territories. I assure you that role will not change, it will only expand, and the Department is committed to helping our country and citizens in time of disaster.

The risk associated with acts of terrorism poses a significant challenge for the Emergency Preparedness and Response Directorate. FEMA's rapid and decisive response to the events of September 11th demonstrated our role in consequence management. As a result, the Nation is looking to the emergency management community to face this new challenge.

Project BioShield was announced by the President in his January 28th State of the Union Address. The doctors on the panel discussed many of the program's specific details, so I want to limit my comments to a few brief statements.

Our Director has the direct responsibility to do a couple of things: One, allow the Federal Government to purchase critically needed vaccines or medication for biodefense. There is $900 million in permanent indefinite authority in the President's 2004 budget.

Two, ensure the adequacy of the Nation's stockpiles of pharmaceutical, vaccines and other medical supplies that can be delivered to emergency sites in 12 hours or less. $400 million are proposed in the President's 2004 budget for this.

And, third, to remove the barriers to the development and production processes, the Department of Homeland Security's role is to do three things: One, serve as the national incident manager coordinating the preparedness and response to any incident that overwhelms or has the potential to overwhelm the resources of State and local government as declared by the President.

We will also work with the Department of Health and Human Services to jointly determine that adequate countermeasures do not exist for a particular threat without the use of BioShield authorities.

Third, along with the FDA, the Department of Homeland Security must declare that chemical, biological, radiological or a nuclear threat is real and requires the use of the BioShield provisions. For this intelligent assessment, we will be looking to the Information Analysis and Information Protectorate Directorate within the Department of Homeland Security.

In short, Homeland Security will coordinate with Health and Human Services to trigger the use of BioShield. We will fund the program's activities and will make a product available through the Strategic National Stockpile.

I am committed to working closely with the various components of the Department of Health and Human Services as they identify the contracting and procurement mechanisms within the pharmaceutical industry, as they work to certify the safety and efficacy of developing new medicines, and as they make recommendations for programmatic progress in areas of needed improvement.

As the custodian of these significant Federal dollars, the Department of Homeland Security is committed to working closely with Health and Human Services to make sure that BioShield authorities are triggered after its use is determined in the Nation's best interest.

Emergency Preparedness and Response is assuming the responsibility for several biopreparedness activities, including developing a bioterrorism response plan called Bio-Watch, participating in the Metropolitan Washington Council of Government's Bioterrorism Task Force, and participating in major bioterrorism response exercises such as TOPOFF 2 and Exercise Silent Night.

First, Emergency Preparedness and Response has assumed the responsibility of maintaining and deploying the Strategic National Stockpile together with the Center for Disease Control and Prevention. The Strategic National Stockpile is made up of pharmaceuticals, vaccines and medical supplies housed in various areas around the country in cases of emergency. By dispersing these assets, the goal is to deliver the necessary supplies to disaster sites in 12 hours or less.

Bio-Watch, which we have talked about, is also included in the responsibilities of Homeland Security and is our effort to make sure that we are ahead of the game in case of emergencies.

The Metropolitan Washington Council on Government's Bioterrorism Task Force is another area that we are working in, including the exercise that we have done in TOPOFF and Silent Night.

The National Disaster Medical System I have already mentioned is also a responsibility assumed by the Department of Homeland

Security under the act. This system assists State and local governments by providing primary care to disaster victims in the field, patient evacuation disaster areas, and definitive care when needed. Our Federal partners include the Departments of Health and Human Services, Defense and Veterans Affairs.

While I have not limited my remarks to BioShield, I think it gives you a good overview of our responsibility in the Department of Homeland Security. We are happy to work in this area and are pleased to answer any questions the committee may have at the close of these opening remarks.

Chairman TOM DAVIS. Well, thank you very much.

[The prepared statement of Mr. Brown follows:]

Michael D. Brown
Undersecretary
Emergency Preparedness and Response Directorate
Department of Homeland Security

Hearing Before
The Committee on Government Reform
United States House of Representatives

"Project BioShield Act of 2003"

April 4, 2003

Good morning Mr. Chairman and Members of the Committee; I am Michael Brown, Undersecretary for the Emergency Preparedness and Response Directorate (EP&R) of the Department of Homeland Security.

I am honored to appear before you today on behalf of Department of Homeland Security Secretary Tom Ridge to discuss our Department's role in bio-terrorism preparedness in general, and BioShield specifically. Having served as the Deputy Director of the Federal Emergency Management Agency and as the Agency's lead on the Department of Homeland Security Transition Team, I am eager to begin my work implementing the many priorities established by Congress and the Administration for the EP&R Directorate. Preparing our citizens for a bio-terrorism event is one of the significant challenges the Department faces.

The Emergency Preparedness and Response Directorate:

I want to provide you some background about the Emergency Preparedness and Response Directorate, its Response Division, and our role in the Department. We are proud to join the Department, and I want to assure the Members of this Committee that EP&R will not lose sight of its main responsibility of helping people and communities affected by disasters. The mission statement of EP&R,

> "To lead the Nation to prepare for, mitigate the effects of, respond to, and recover from major domestic disasters, both natural and man-made, including acts of terrorism,"

contains the same core responsibilities that guided the Federal Emergency Management Agency (FEMA) as an independent Agency.

The Response Division coordinates and implements the federal response to Presidentially declared disasters. During FY 2002, FEMA expended nearly $3.9 billion in disaster funds to aid people and communities overwhelmed by disasters, which included earthquakes, floods, ice and winter storms, fires, hurricanes, tornadoes, and tropical storms. FEMA responded to 42 major disasters involving 37 States and 4 U.S. Territories.

The Response Division is charged with developing and maintaining an integrated, nationwide operational capability to respond to and recover from disasters and emergencies, regardless of their cause, in partnership with other Federal agencies, State and local governments, volunteer organizations, and the private sector.

The risks associated with acts of terrorism pose a significant challenge for EP&R. FEMA's rapid and decisive response to the events of September 11 demonstrated the Agency's role in consequence management. As a result, the Nation is looking to the emergency management community—and EP&R in particular—to face this challenge. Augmenting and maintaining the Strategic National Stockpile, and strengthening their future capacity, to ensure there are adequate supplies in the event of a national emergency are important steps in meeting the challenge.

Project BioShield

In his State of the Union Address, President Bush announced Project BioShield as an effort to develop and make available modern, effective medical countermeasures, especially vaccines and anti-toxins to protect against a biological or chemical weapon, or other dangerous pathogens. This new Project will be built on the many health advances in basic medical science and pharmaceutical manufacturing technology that our society has enjoyed in recent years.

Specifically, Project BioShield will ensure that the resources are made available to pay for advanced development and large-scale acquisition of "next-generation" medical countermeasures as soon as scientists can assert that the envisioned countermeasure is reasonably likely to be licensable, and that large-scale manufacturing of a safe and effective product is reasonably feasible, within the near term. President Bush has proposed creating a permanent indefinite funding authority to spur development of medical countermeasures. This authority will help ensure that the private sector contributes to this effort by ensuring them that if they can produce a needed countermeasure, the government can and will purchase it.

Second, Project BioShield will strengthen the capabilities of the National Institutes of Health (NIH) by expediting research and development on medical countermeasures based on promising, recent scientific discoveries. The new authorities provided to NIH would apply only to support research and development of biomedical countermeasures against bioterrorism threat agents. Funding of grants and contracts will remain subject to rigorous scientific and peer review, but expedited peer review procedures could be used when appropriate.

Finally, Project BioShield will enable the Food and Drug Administration (FDA) to make promising treatments available in emergency situations if alternative treatments are not available. This authority is not intended to alter the FDA's thorough review before licensing a product. Rather, BioShield authorities will supplement the traditional FDA licensing process to ensure that we could respond effectively in a crisis to use medical countermeasures that experts have judged safe and effective. These countermeasures will be subject to Government controls, and can only be used after certain certifications have been made. Furthermore, all civilian use would be voluntary and the benefits of the treatment in question to be used in an emergency situation must outweigh the expected risks.

We must continue to encourage scientific initiative and creativity to ensure rewards for innovators who bring needed countermeasures to the American public. And, the breakthroughs resulting from Project BioShield are likely to have important spillover benefits in preventing and treating other diseases, and in strengthening our overall biotechnology infrastructure.

The Department of Homeland Security is working closely with the Department of Health and Human Services and the Department of Veterans Affairs, as those entities are equipped to identify contracting and procurement issues with the pharmaceutical industry; to assess when new countermeasures can be made that will be safe and effective; and to make recommendations for programmatic progress and areas of improvement. EP&R will be responsible for the Department's role as proprietor of the budget authority under BioShield (we estimate the use of nearly $900 million in the President's FY 2004 Budget) to allow the federal government to purchase critically needed vaccines or medication for biodefense, and to ensure the adequacy of the nation's stockpiles of pharmaceutical, vaccine and other medical supplies, and to promote removal of barriers to the development and production processes.

Emergency Preparedness and Response Bio-preparedness Activities

The Department of Homeland Security's work in the bio-preparedness arena includes developing an environmental surveillance system and associated response plans; the Bio-Watch surveillance program; participating in Metropolitan Washington Council of Governments Bio-terrorism Task force; and participating in major bio-terrorism response exercises such as TOPOFF 2 and Exercise Silent Night.

As one of its responsibilities, EP&R has assumed responsibility for the National Disaster Medical System (NDMS). This system assists State and local governments by providing primary care to disaster victims in the field, patient evacuation from disaster areas, and definitive care, when needed. The three other federal partners for NDMS are the Departments of Health and Human Services, Defense and Veterans Affairs.

NDMS is a nationwide medical response system to supplement State and local medical resources during disasters and emergencies and to provide backup medical support during an overseas conflict. The System is activated in response to all-hazards, thus preparing the teams to respond to any event including a terrorist event that may be chemical, biological or nuclear in nature.

EP&R has also assumed the responsibility, together with the Centers for Disease Control and Prevention, of maintaining and deploying the Strategic National Stockpile. The President's budget for Fiscal Year 2004 includes a request for $400 million to maintain the Strategic National Stockpile. The Strategic National Stockpile is made up of pharmaceuticals, vaccines and medical supplies housed in various areas around the country in case of emergencies. By dispersing the assets, the necessary supplies can be delivered to any disaster site within 12 hours. Once development and production of needed pharmaceuticals and vaccines is completed through BioShield, these new items may be placed in the Strategic National Stockpile.

Bio-Watch, an inter-agency initiative involving the Department of Homeland Security, Department of Energy, the Department of Defense, and the Environmental Protection Agency, is developing sophisticated air monitoring and analysis systems to detect large-scale releases of biological agents. Our role is to develop response plans that are more pro-active and responsive in managing the consequences of a biological or chemical attack.

The Metropolitan Washington Council on Governments' Bioterrorism Task Force provides a national model for integrated bio-terrorism response planning. The effort focusing on the National Capital Region provides a structure for Federal, State, local, private sector and cross-jurisdictional coordination, communication, and effective detection and response.

Finally, EP&R is working closely with other federal agencies, State and local contacts on two significant bioterrorism Exercises: The Top Officials 2 (TOPOFF 2 Exercise), schedule for this spring, is a major counter-terrorism exercise focusing on the nations response to bioterrorism. Participation in TOPOFF 2 and other bioterrorism exercises enables the response elements to be better prepared to deal with a terrorist attack involving biological, chemical or radiological weapons

Closing

While I have not limited my remarks to BioShield, I hope this information provides you sufficient background on our work to prepare this Nation in the event of a biological attack. I would be pleased to answer any questions the Committee members may have.

Chairman TOM DAVIS. Dr. Klein.

Dr. KLEIN. Chairman Davis, distinguished members of the committee, I am pleased to be provided the opportunity to appear before you today. As indicated, my name is Dale Klein; and I currently serve as Assistant Secretary of Defense for Nuclear, Chemical and Biological Defense Programs.

Within the Department of Defense, I have the responsibility for all matters concerning the formulation of policy and plans for nuclear, chemical and biological defense programs. In this role, I am responsible for the Department of Defense programs to develop and field biological countermeasures our warfighting forces need.

Due to the support of Congress and with the help of the resources you have made available to the Department, our fighters that are now in the vicinity of Baghdad are much more prepared than they were in 1991 under Operation Desert Storm.

The Department of Defense is very interested in the prompt approval of the administration's Project BioShield initiative. New authorities are needed with appropriate safeguards to assure rapid and effective medical treatments can be introduced quickly to counter weapons of mass destruction. The President's Project BioShield initiative would enhance the Food and Drug administration's ability to make needed medical products available in response to declaration of an emergency.

DOD stands ready to assist civilian agencies in their efforts to provide modern, effective drugs and vaccines to protect against attack by biological, chemical, nuclear or radiological weapons.

The Department looks forward to working closely with Congress, the Department of Health and Human Services and the Department of Homeland Security to collaborate as the lessons of the 2001 anthrax attacks are fresh in our minds.

Currently, we are working with the Department of Health and Human Services and other Federal agencies to develop the next generation anthrax vaccines for future use and several other programs.

Mr. Chairman, in summary, I request that my full statement be placed in the record; and I want to reemphasize that the Department of Defense supports the President's Project BioShield initiative.

I will be happy to answer questions you may have later. Thank you.

Chairman TOM DAVIS. Well, thank you very much.

[The prepared statement of Dr. Klein follows:]

FOR OFFICIAL USE ONLY
UNTIL RELEASED BY THE
HOUSE GOVERNMENT REFORM COMMITTEE

STATEMENT OF

DR. DALE KLEIN

ASSISTANT TO THE SECRETARY OF DEFENSE FOR NUCLEAR AND CHEMICAL AND BIOLOGICAL DEFENSE PROGRAMS

BEFORE THE

HOUSE GOVERNMENT REFORM COMMITTEE

U.S. HOUSE OF REPRESENTATIVES

PROJECT BIO SHIELD

APRIL 4, 2003

FOR OFFICIAL USE ONLY
UNTIL RELEASED BY THE
HOUSE GOVERNMENT REFORM COMMITTEE

Statement of Dr. Dale Klein,
Assistant to the Secretary of Defense for
Nuclear and Chemical, and Biological Defense Programs
Before the House Government Reform Committee
U.S. House of Representatives
Project Bio Shield

Chairman and Distinguished Committee Members, I was appointed to my present position by President Bush in November 2001, following the advice and consent of the Senate Within the Department of Defense, I have responsibility for all matters concerning the formulation of policy and plans for nuclear, chemical and biological defense programs. In this role, I am responsible for the DoD programs to develop and field the biological countermeasures our warfighting force needs. I am the focal point for the oversight, coordination and integration of the Department's medical and non-medical chemical and biological defense research, development, and acquisition efforts. I want to assure the committee that the Department's Chemical Biological Defense Program is a top priority for the senior leadership of the Department and the Services. Due to the support of the Congress and with the help of the resources you have made available to the Department; our fighting forces are equipped and trained far better than in 1991 during OPERATION DESERT STORM.

We are very interested in prompt approval of the Administration's Project BioShield initiative. New authorities are needed, with appropriate safeguards, to assure rapid and effective medical treatments can be introduced quickly to counter weapons of mass destruction. The President's Project BioShield initiative would enhance the Food and Drug Administration's ability to make needed medical products available in response to declaration of an emergency issued by the Secretary of Health and Human Services that is based on findings by the Secretary, the Secretary of Homeland Security, or the Secretary of Defense.

DoD has many years of experience in areas covered by the Bill and we stand ready to assist the civilian agencies in their efforts to provide modern, effective drugs and vaccines to protect against attack by biological, chemical, nuclear and radiological weapons. The Department looks forward to working closely with the Congress, the DHHS and DHS to collaborate as required to improve our preparedness.

The DoD Joint Chemical Biological Defense Program's initiatives over the last decade have significantly improved our ability to protect Service members from the effects of chemical and biological weapons. Initiatives have resulted in improvements in the whole family of chemical and biological defense systems, including improved detection and identification technologies, improved individual protection systems, improved decontaminants, and improved medical protection against potential chemical and biological agents. The research funded by the Department is providing essential information that can lead to even higher levels of protection for our forces in medical detection, surveillance, prevention, and treatment. In today's age, this research also has applicability for all of our citizens and our allies. For example, the Department is working in collaboration with the Centers for Disease Control and Prevention (CDC) and the National Institute of Allergy and Infectious Diseases (NIAID) in researching antivirals and other countermeasures to smallpox and other pathogens.

We continue to work in close consultation and coordination with agencies across the federal government, as we make significant advances in protecting our military forces against the biological weapons threat. We are working with DHHS and other federal agencies to develop a next generation anthrax vaccine for future use. Recent funding provided to the NIAID has stimulated coordination and cooperation with the DoD medical biological defense research program. Initiatives are under way for close collaboration between scientists in both organizations.

Mr. Chairman, in summation I want to re-emphasize that the Department supports the President's Project BioShield initiative- a comprehensive effort to develop and make available modern, effective drugs and vaccines to protect against attack by biological and chemical weapons or other dangerous pathogens. We believe that Project BioShield has the potential to provide mutual benefits and advances for DoD personnel, the American public, and our allies. By bringing researchers, medical experts, and the biomedical industry together in a new and focused way, our Nation can achieve new breakthroughs for biological medical defense.

Chairman TOM DAVIS. I want to thank all of the panelists.

We are going to start the questions. I just have a quick question before I yield to Mr. Waxman, and then we will get another round.

Dr. Fauci, next week this committee is going to be holding a hearing on the Severe Acute Respiratory Syndrome [SARS] epidemic. Can you give us an update on what we now know about SARS, including how it is transmitted, how far it has spread and what we can do to protect ourselves?

Dr. FAUCI. Certainly, Mr. Chairman.

SARS, standing for Severe Acute Respiratory Syndrome, has now spread through several countries, at least 17 countries. There are over 2,200 cases, and about 80 deaths. There has now been 100 cases in the United States in 27 States.

This is a new disease. It is what we refer to as an emerging microbe, an emerging infectious disease. The data from the CDC and from other laboratories indicate that the corona virus, which is an interesting group—it is a very common virus. It is what causes about 10 to 20 percent of the common colds. There are two groups of corona viruses. This is likely a member of a new third group. It has not been definitively demonstrated that this is the, or the only, cause of SARS, but the evidence is mounting every day from a variety of approaches that we are taking.

It has the capability of being a very severe syndrome. The death rate in this is 3.5 percent, which may sound small, but when you think about the possibility of infecting hundreds of millions of people, this can turn out to be a major public health threat. In fact, in parts of the world it already is, leading to such draconian measures as quarantines and isolation in several countries.

The CDC has done a magnificent job thus far, and we know that they will continue to, in not only identifying and tracking but essentially now moving ahead in collaboration with the NIH and a variety of other agencies, the FDA, in developing diagnostic therapeutics and on our way to a vaccine.

So, in summary, Mr. Chairman, it is a serious threat. We must take it very seriously. We don't feel there is a need to panic at this point, but we must continue to do the very stringent public health measures that we are approaching, as well as the research that is going into it.

Chairman TOM DAVIS. Thank you. That is just a synopsis. We will have a fuller hearing next week with more questions. But thank you for that.

Let me yield to our ranking member, Mr. Waxman.

Mr. WAXMAN. Thank you very much, Mr. Chairman. That was very interesting, what you had to say about this SARS. Our committee is going to hold a hearing on it next week. I think it is important for us to understand this very looming threat to the public and how best to deal with it.

On this BioShield proposal, the administration is suggesting that NIH conduct a research and development program for biological countermeasures. It then authorizes the procurement of countermeasures but only after determinations by the Secretary of HHS and Homeland Security and Presidential approval. But, Dr. Fauci, who makes the decisions about the research and development phase?

Dr. FAUCI. We do, sir; and that is the point that I alluded to briefly in my opening remarks. There is the push and the pull. The NIH and other research agencies make a scientific decision about the kinds of research that we need to do. We rely heavily, as others do, on intelligence reports, particularly from the new Department of Homeland Security about the threat assessment. But the fundamental basic research, that is our decision; and the way we execute this research is a scientific decision.

Mr. WAXMAN. You will be making decisions about research into countermeasures at the same time you oversee research against present threats to health.

Dr. FAUCI. Yes, sir.

Mr. WAXMAN. Should Congress be worried that traditional medical research will slow down as NIH focuses on biodefense?

Dr. FAUCI. I don't believe so, Mr. Waxman. There is always a concern when you have to rev up and ratchet up your activities that there will be resources taken away from other areas, but if you look now thus far at the track record of the providing of resources for biodefense at the NIH, it has been quite extraordinary. We appreciate not only the administration but the Congress and their bipartisan support of that.

But if you look at the other areas of the naturally emerging and reemerging diseases, that has not suffered and in fact has grown at a rate commensurate with the rather substantial growth of the rest of the NIH. So, in fact, we have not seen that.

Mr. WAXMAN. Is there a potential for dual use where the research of biodefense may well lead us to research breakthroughs for other diseases?

Dr. FAUCI. I think it is not only a potential, Mr. Waxman, I think it is inevitable that there will be an important contribution to the research that we put into emerging and reemerging diseases to inform us about biodefense research, and it is without a doubt that the research that goes into biodefense will help us with naturally occurring.

Because as a matter of fact, as we have discussed before, as you know we feel that deliberately released microbes is just another form of emerging and reemerging disease. Instead of occurring naturally, it is done with malice and deliberately, but the end result can be the same.

In some respects, nature itself can be our worst bioterrorist. So the resources and the manpower and the expertise that goes into one will naturally flow seamlessly back and forth into the other.

Mr. WAXMAN. Let me ask you about antibiotic resistance. This certainly poses a threat to public health now and a potential bioterrorist threat for the future. Yet drug companies have few antibiotics in development, and some people believe there is a market failure for drugs to treat resistant bacteria. How urgent is the crisis in antibiotic resistance and does it make sense for BioShield to cover research into new antibiotics to treat resistant bacteria?

Dr. FAUCI. The answer to your question is it is a serious threat, and it has been a threat for some time. I think you alluded to, in your opening statement, the fact that, you know, as months go by, we are pushing the envelope further and further about the emergence of resistance to microbes for which we have maybe one last firewall of an antibiotic against that.

We are recognizing this at the research level, and we are putting more resources into it. But I believe, and we all believe, that the basic research that we will be doing on microbes for biodefense will directly and indirectly address the concerns that you have and the concerns that we have.

For example, as part of our biodefense research endeavor, we are involved in a major program for the sequencing of pathogenic microbes, not only those on the category A or B list, but microbes for which one can, by a simple mutation, lead to a microbe that would be a bioterror weapon.

So that kind of research that we have been doing before in emerging and reemerging disease research and that we have accelerated greatly with biodefense will address the question you are concerned about.

Mr. WAXMAN. As you know, our vaccine infrastructure is very fragile, and we always have to be concerned about the vaccines for childhood diseases. Do you see any potential where the efforts to develop and produce bioterror vaccines could negatively impact childhood vaccine capabilities?

Dr. FAUCI. I don't think it would negatively do that at all. In fact, if we can, which I hope that we do, that the long-range effect would be to add a degree of robustness and vigor to the whole field of vaccinology, that there will be positive spin-offs.

You are quite correct. We are walking a very thin line, notwithstanding biodefense in the whole field of vaccinology, because of so few companies that are involved for a variety of reasons.

We feel that if we get both the basic research and the actual production flow of vaccines in general that this will have positive spinoffs on vaccines for childhood diseases as well as adult nonbiodefense vaccines.

Mr. WAXMAN. Thank you very much.

Dr. McClellan, the BioShield proposal would allow the Secretary of Health and Human Services to waive virtually all of the consumer protections in the Federal Food and Drug Cosmetic Act in case of an emergency. Moreover, the proposal would then severely curtail judicial review of the Secretary's decision. What is the rationale for allowing informed consent, recordkeeping, adverse event reporting, and other key requirements to be waived; and what is the rationale for severely limiting oversight of these extraordinary powers?

Dr. MCCLELLAN. The rationale for the emergency use authorization is to provide the most potentially effective treatments to Americans in emergency situations. This is a limited authority program that only applies when the Secretary and others have determined there is a national emergency because of a bioterrorism threat or another type of public health emergency, and it only involves agents where there are not effective approved treatments already available but where there may be treatments in the pipeline where the potential benefits outweigh the potential risks. We have a few now that are marching as quickly as possible toward approval and toward a full demonstration of safety and effectiveness. That remains our goal.

I would highlight that we are going to have even better incentives for that under the BioShield program. You don't get full payment for development of a countermeasure under BioShield unless it is approved and licensed, fully licensed, fully shown to be safe and effective by the FDA. That is a strong incentive for getting to the finish line that doesn't exist today and would move us out of the world we are in now, where there are a lot of products that may be of use, but no companies, as I talked about before, are willing to make the investments and come up with the good ideas needed to translate proof of concept into a truly effective treatment.

Mr. WAXMAN. I understand that. That is an important part of why this bill is necessary. But in creating this balance we let the Secretary waive all of these consumer protections, and it looks to me like this authority is quite broad to waive FDA approval standards. Will that give incentives that are needed to conduct the kinds of safety and efficacy trials that are needed, or are some of these companies going to figure they can get around that?

Dr. MCCLELLAN. I agree we need more incentives to conduct the needed safety and effectiveness trials. That is the main reason for the procurement authority for BioShield that only makes payment on delivery of—a full payment for an approved product.

The emergency use authorization does include a number of protections to make sure that in the limited circumstances of the emergency we do as much as possible to limit distrubution, limit who can administer, require studies, require recordkeeping and access to records. All of those are elements of the BioShield proposal, and the Secretary would specifically design its use with our recommendations and those of others to do as much of all of those activities as possible.

Mr. WAXMAN. You are giving me assurances that we are not going to pay these companies unless they do what they are required to do, but I am concerned about the broad authority to waive some of the consumer protections like informed consent or making sure we know about the adverse events and other aspects, where right now the law is set up to not just make sure the company does what it needs to do to get paid but the consumers and adverse consequences—the consumers are monitored with and dealt with adequately.

Dr. MCCLELLAN. Right. We want to get to approved treatments as quickly as possible. But with these products in development there may be a number that have been shown to have potential benefits for conditions where there are no effective treatments approved. Under those circumstances, we think it is appropriate, with all of these restrictions in place, to do as much recordkeeping as possible, as much monitoring and standards for production as possible, as much mandatory reporting of adverse events, and informing the consumer, informing the public as possible about appropriate use as can be done under the circumstances. I would be happy to continue to work with your staff to make sure that we tailor that language appropriately.

We think the bill does a pretty good job now of getting as much done as possible on informing consumers, on collecting adverse event data and the like. We think that is very important in the emergency use process. But it is an emergency, and it is a very special limited use condition that requires some special considerations.

Mr. WAXMAN. Your answer is very useful. I have other questions, but we will pursue them in a subsequent round. I appreciate your offer to work with us to improve the bill.

Mr. SHAYS [presiding]. As the ranking member points out, we will have a second round.

What we are doing is we are doing 5-minute doubles, so we are doing a 10-minute questioning period. I will recognize myself.

I would like to ask each of you, what is your assessment of the seriousness of the threat we face with bioterrorism? Just start with you, Dr. Fauci.

Dr. FAUCI. I think the threat is serious. The risk of it happening is something that we can't quantify. But if one looks at the history of what has gone on in the production of weapons of bioterrorism decades ago, that we have no real assurance of their full accountability, for example, by the Soviet Union, the recognition of weapons of bioterror that were clearly recovered in the first Gulf war, and right now obviously we need to see what happens in the current engagements.

The fact that we have already been hit in the fall of 2001 and the potential for this has us feel strongly that we need to err very strongly on the side of preparedness. So it is difficult to quantify a risk, but we are concerned.

Mr. SHAYS. Dr. McClellan.

Dr. MCCLELLAN. I agree with that assessment. There is a real reason for concern.

In addition to the specific risk that Dr. Fauci has outlined, I would like to highlight that, as part of our preparedness efforts, we have already undertaken a number of threat assessments and at FDA we have got responsibility for the security of most of the food supply.

As Secretary Thompson has said, he is very concerned about the real risk of bioterrorists or other type of terrorist events involving foods. I would like to highlight that it is not only bioterrorism that we are concerned about here. Recently discovered terrorist cells in Europe that were attempting to manufacture Ricin and previous episodes of cyanide poisoning highlight that various chemical agents also pose a real risk to the health of the public.

Mr. SHAYS. Mr. Brown.

Mr. BROWN. I want to emphasize what Dr. McClellan just said, the threat is real. But I want to add a different dimension to it. Even if terrorists are not successful in launching a wide-scale biological attack or a chemical attack, they will launch a small-scale attack, just for the effect, for the terror effect alone. So that even if they don't infect a wide, broad spectrum of society, if they can put the fear in the American public that they have this capability, by launching a small attack somewhere, they will do that.

Mr. Chairman, it is real.

Mr. SHAYS. Dr. Klein.

Dr. KLEIN. Mr. Chairman, I would also like to acknowledge that the threat is real and serious. I think the events of September 11th demonstrated that. The anthrax attacks also demonstrated that.

The Department of Defense has a fairly significant monitoring program; and I think, on the biological threat side, one of the reasons that is a concern is the capital investment to produce those materials are less than it would cost to develop, for example, a nuclear weapon.

Mr. SHAYS. I am going to work backward, Dr. Klein. We will go the other way. What do you think the future of bioweapons will be? Should we focus mostly on natural pathogens or enhanced pathogens? And what enhancements to these pathogens should concern us most?

Dr. KLEIN. Well, Mr. Chairman, I think when we look at what specific threats we look at, we have a process, both at the Department of Defense and with our interagency colleagues, to define what those threats are. So we have a process to evaluate those specific threats.

What we look at at the Department of Defense, for our men and women in uniform, we look at not only what is it that might be available but what can be weaponized.

I think my colleagues at the Department of Homeland Security and the Department of Health and Human Services have other areas where the terror threats would be different. So I think what we need to do collectively, and I think BioShield addresses this, is that we need to work collectively as an interagency to define those threats.

Mr. SHAYS. Just quickly. The other part of the question, though, is it the natural pathogen or the enhanced pathogens, in other words, the altered biological agent?

Dr. KLEIN. In my opinion, in the near term, it will be the natural ones that have been modified for a weapon. Then we will look at the modified ones.

Mr. SHAYS. Mr. Brown.

Mr. BROWN. Based on the intelligence I have been receiving and looking at, I think it is the natural pathogens, those that they can use quickly and easily.

Mr. SHAYS. Dr. McClellan.

Dr. MCCLELLAN. We rely on the Department of Homeland Security and others for help with these threat assessments, so I defer to them. I do think we need to be prepared for both types of agents, both naturally occurring and modified ones.

Some of the technologies that we have outlined that we think would result from a BioShield initiative such as monoclonal antibody techniques and better techniques for producing vaccines quickly will support our ability to deal with modified pathogens as well as the naturally occurring ones. So the approach that we are outlining here would provide a useful strategy for addressing both.

I would like to emphasize again, though, that the only threats out there are not bioweapon agents. Also, chemical agents and radiologic and nuclear agents are real threats, too.

Mr. SHAYS. Thank you.

Dr. Fauci.

Dr. FAUCI. I agree with my copanelists' statements. We also rely heavily on the Department of Homeland Security for threat assessment. But the strategic plan and research agenda for the NIH is weighted to both naturally occurring as well as genetically modified microbes.

Mr. SHAYS. Dr. McClellan, I will start with you and work to Mr. Brown. How many medical countermeasures, diagnostic drugs and vaccines do you estimate we will need in the end to protect ourselves?

Dr. MCCLELLAN. I can't give you a specific number. One of the things that comes out of the threat assessments and that will come out of our work under BioShield is a much clearer assessment of what is possible.

Mr. SHAYS. When will that be?

Dr. MCCLELLAN. By passing this legislation we will generate a higher level of interest among the private sector researchers and others in identifying countermeasures.

We have identified a number that we think can be developed right away, including better treatments for smallpox, better treatments for botulism, better treatments for anthrax. But we think there are a lot of other opportunities out there, so I can't give you an exact number.

But I do think that, because this is an unexplored and really underutilized area——

Mr. SHAYS. You have explained. I want to move on.

Mr. Brown.

Mr. BROWN. Homeland security has to rely on their expertise for those kinds of matters.

Mr. SHAYS. OK. You have no sense.

Dr. Klein.

Dr. KLEIN. It is difficult to say exactly which numbers. I agree with my colleague, Dr. McClellan, it is difficult to come up with an exact number. But we will—if we have a system in place that can be versatile, I think that is what would protect the American public.

Mr. SHAYS. OK. The Defense Science Board listed 19 priority bioterror agents.

First, Dr. Fauci, would you just respond to the question, and then I want—the question I started with Dr. McClellan. The question is, how many medical countermeasures, diagnostic drugs and vaccines do you estimate?

Dr. FAUCI. Difficult to assess. But we are at least aiming at the six high-priority category A and several on the category B list. So I would say the number we cannot tell you for sure, but we want to be flexible enough to move as new threats arise.

Mr. SHAYS. OK. I will ask whoever can answer this. The Defense Science Board listed 19 priority bioterror agents, and found that today we have none of the diagnostics we need, none of the vaccines we need, and only one of the therapeutics we need to deal with them. Is this list of 19 pathogens the definitive list, or do we need to prepare for these and many other pathogens, some of which don't even exist yet?

Dr. KLEIN. As you might expect on that list, we do have some vaccines available. For example, anthrax is on the list, smallpox is on the list. So we do have vaccines and treatments available. We need to continue those. That list is relatively accurate but, again, as others have indicated, there will be future threats that are not on that list.

Mr. SHAYS. CDC list, 36 selected agents. Do we need countermeasures for all of them? Dr. Fauci.

Dr. FAUCI. Potentially we do. We are using that list which includes the top priority category A list of six that we are putting our major effort on, but there are several on the secondary or B or C lists that we are also developing countermeasures, or at least studying the basic biology of the microbes to prepare us better in case genetically modified microbes appear.

Mr. SHAYS. Let me just ask about the issue of surveillance diagnostic tools and training medical personnel. Isn't that more important than any of the stuff that we are talking about right now, to be able to have a surveillance system and diagnostic tools and training medical personnel? Do these come first?

Dr. MCCLELLAN. It is all part of a comprehensive strategy with dealing with the new threats of terrorism to this country. We need effective surveillance and supporting research on better diagnostic techniques as well as building up our laboratory and monitoring capabilities is an important part of the response, but so is research on developing effective countermeasures and strategies for containing an event if it actually occurs.

Mr. SHAYS. Anybody disagree with that?

Dr. FAUCI. Agree.

Mr. SHAYS. Let me just ask this one last question then. We are in a dangerous position with regard to antibiotics and have few antivirals. Do we need some major research breakthroughs to develop products that we need to protect ourselves against a bioterror attack and antibiotic-resistant organisms?

Dr. FAUCI. The answer is yes. That is a problem, as I mentioned in response to Mr. Waxman's question, and it is an important part of our biodefense program in general as well as our nonbiodefense emerging and re-emerging disease, which I believe shows you the seamlessness between the two programs.

Mr. SHAYS. In my second round I want to ask about the DOD joint vaccine acquisition, and I will be asking you, Dr. Fauci, some questions and Dr. Klein about that.

And, Mr. Van Hollen, you have the floor for 10 minutes.

Mr. VAN HOLLEN. Welcome to all of you, and I am very proud to have both the NIH and the FDA in the Eighth Congressional District, so it is great to see both of you and have a chance to visit with you. I appreciate your willingness to work with our office on not just national issues, but some of the local issues as well.

Much ground has been covered, but I want to followup on a couple of things just so I am clear in my mind. The determination as to what the priorities are going to be in terms of what—whether it is biological weapons, chemical weapons, which ones we focus on as a priority, is that decision—I understand it is part of a collaborative process, but is it part of the Department of Homeland Security to say that these are the ones we want to focus on? Who is responsible for making that decision as to what the priorities are for investing resources?

Dr. KLEIN. Congressman, I think what happens in that regard is that we—both the Department of Defense and Department of

Homeland Security will both work together to determine those. Sometimes they are slightly different. What the Department of Defense considers is not only the threat, but has it been weaponized to negatively impact the men and women in uniform accomplishing their mission.

What we do, we will come up with that threat list. We will evaluate it through our intelligence system. Certainly as we develop those lists, we will work with the Department of Homeland Security. But which list is more important than others, it depends on exactly what your mission is, for example, whether it is a warfighting mission or protecting civilians.

Mr. VAN HOLLEN. I assume we are going to be putting together a plan. What is your time line in terms of deciding—there are a lot of chemical agents out there. There are lots of potential biological agents, a lot of different mutations, I understand. What are we——

Dr. KLEIN. We already have that list, and it is prioritized. We have them ranked. We typically don't publicize that list at the Department of Defense.

Mr. VAN HOLLEN. You have that list, and NIH is doing research based on that list?

Dr. KLEIN. The Department of Homeland Security and Department of Health and Human Services also have a list, and their list, Department of HHS, their list A and B, and it is publicized.

Mr. VAN HOLLEN. Does that also deal with the production of countermeasures as opposed to research? Who makes the decision as to what point we need to move into the actual production of the countermeasures?

Dr. MCCLELLAN. The production is a decision that is made with input from the Department of Health and Human Services based on the threat assessment. Where we ought to focus our resources and BioShield more generally is based on the combination of where the greatest threats are and where the greatest opportunities are, and where you get that match, the potential for bringing new countermeasures forward that will address a significant terrorist threat, that is the priority in BioShield.

Dr. FAUCI. I see where your question is going, because there really needs to be distinguished both the basic fundamental research that informs any list. The decisions about that and how you track that is an NIH decision when it comes to research and FDA or CDC decision in the Department of Heath and Human Services. As we mentioned earlier, we rely heavily on our colleagues in DHS and even in DOD in helping us to get a better feel for the actual threat assessment. However, there is a formal process in BioShield that Dr. McClellan just referred to that when you trigger the procurement component of it, it is the Department of Homeland Security and Secretary Ridge determines that this is a serious threat that we need to have the countermeasure for, and then the Department of Health and Human Services executes the research and public health measures to go into getting that particular countermeasure.

Mr. VAN HOLLEN. Have there been any decisions to date with respect to the need to move forward on the production of any countermeasures?

Dr. KLEIN. In terms of looking at production, we need the R&D to develop a product, and then as soon as that is evaluated, all of our agencies look with the limited resources how can we best meet the threats as we see them. We at the Department of Defense have an anthrax producing program. We work closely with Department of Health and Human Services with the smallpox, for example.

Mr. VAN HOLLEN. I remember at the time there was a lot of questions about whether we had adequate anthrax supplies or not. Other than anthrax and smallpox, have there been any decisions with respect to moving ahead on countermeasures on other agents whether chemical or biological?

Dr. MCCLELLAN. We have worked with the Department of Homeland Security and others to identify some of the immediate opportunities that we think BioShield would help us fulfill even more quickly. So, for example, a better vaccine for anthrax, a better, safer vaccine for smallpox, and better antitoxins for botulinum toxin are all areas where the technology exists, and what's needed is the funding to get companies to follow through to produce the actual products.

Mr. VAN HOLLEN. Thank you, Mr. Chairman. Next round of questions I do have a concern that Mr. Waxman raised with respect to resources—we have limited.

Chairman TOM DAVIS [presiding]. Keep going. You have 5 more minutes.

Mr. VAN HOLLEN. One question. Obviously there are all these possible threats out there, biological, chemical, nuclear. As a Nation we obviously have to evaluate the threat—the level of the threat posed and the likelihood—what kind of damage it will cause, and the likelihood of that threat versus what we know are very known threats that we are facing every day, heart disease and a whole range of medical problems that NIH is engaged in research with right today. And I am concerned that this will—you know, it is one thing to add additional resources to this effort at a time since September 11th, an emergency and a focus on this, but I would hate to see it come at the expense of what we know are diseases that are harming and killing Americans every day.

And so my question is of the amount of resources that is being invested in this effort and research, how much of that is coming out of what otherwise would be invested in nonbiological and chemical research?

Dr. FAUCI. If you look at the resource curve of the last 2 years, which have been heavily weighted in the arena of biodefense, the other areas, in fact, have not suffered. Now, obviously the NIH has gone through a doubling, which it has completed successfully. The next few years, obviously if one looks at what is coming forth as the budget from the administration as was expected, it is not going to continue at that level, it is reaching a point of plateauing. But within the framework of that, again, we have tried as best as possible to not damage the effort and the momentum in other areas. So what has happened thus far with the doubling of the budget has not taken away from other areas. It has been a substantial and very generous increase in NIH's budget.

Dr. MCCLELLAN. I would like to respond to that from the standpoint of product development. After you have done the basic research, approve the concept, is this going to take away from the development of much-needed new products for cancer, heart disease and other priority areas? We have seen over the past decade a huge expansion of the biotech sector, pharmaceutical research and development and so forth. While NIH's budget has been doubling, the research investments in development and applied stages on the private side have also been doubling as well. And what is responsible for that is the potential for some real breakthroughs especially in naturally occurring diseases that the private sector is trying to step up to address. By adding on these additional financial incentives for BioShield, we provide more incentives to get more investment activity, research and development in these other priority areas as well.

As long as the financial incentives are there, the incentives to develop products will be there. We aren't taking away incentives in cancer, heart diseases and naturally occurring diseases. We are correcting a deficiency that exists in these unnatural diseases.

Mr. VAN HOLLEN. Thank you, Mr. Chairman.

Chairman TOM DAVIS. Thank you very much.

I have a question for the panel. Do you consider the acquisition flexibilities that are contained in the Senate bill, do you think they provide adequate incentives to spur the development and supply of critical countermeasures?

Dr. MCCLELLAN. We do think that they would provide some much-needed incentives. Obviously there have been some different views expressed about what's needed to actually bring these next-generation products to the public, and we are absolutely willing to work with this committee and other experts on making sure we have the right framework in place to do that.

I do think the most critical element's there, making sure that there's a certainty of payment, sometimes years in advance, if an effective, highly valuable product is actually developed, approved and delivered for use by the public in the event of a terrorist or other emergency health threat.

Chairman TOM DAVIS. There is a consensus here that we just don't have the in House capability to take this in government and do it by ourselves. Everyone agree with that? There is no way we could build that up in a short period of time. So we are by necessity forced to go to the private sector to incentivize them to do things they otherwise wouldn't do.

Dr. FAUCI. Of which they do very, very well. They do it very, very well.

Dr. MCCLELLAN. It's not easy to develop a product that is safe and effective and reliably produced even after you have gotten through the basic research and have a proof of concept. There is a lot of testing that needs to be done of potential toxicities that need to be determined in each individual case. There is effectiveness testing, which is particularly challenging in this area because you can't do normal testing on humans. And there are all kinds of challenges to getting ramped efficient production, labeling and delivery of the product. These are things that the private sector does extremely well in many other areas of medical technology, and we have seen the benefits of that for the public. We haven't seen the same kinds of benefit here, and we need them.

Chairman TOM DAVIS. I guess one of the differences we have is—in the next panel, we are going to hear concerns that the BioShield does not really afford manufacturers of the biomedical countermeasures enough protection against product liability lawsuits. Obviously they are going to be engaging in research and development and manufacture of things they wouldn't do otherwise. We are trying to get them to do it. If they are exposed to massive lawsuits, it could bring the company down, expose the rest of their business. I don't know what the right balance is. That is something we need to try to find. And the companies, I think, are trying to get as much protection as they can. Anybody have a feel for the right balance here?

Dr. MCCLELLAN. As a general matter, the administration has expressed some concerns about problems of liability exposures for manufacturers creating roadblocks to developing needed new treatments, and in this case it is something that we all need to think carefully about. We believe that there's a lot that can be done under authority, Section 85–804 authorities, that we have and under the Safety Act to provide protection for manufacturers for products that are being purchased by the government and used in these emergency situations. But obviously this is an issue that needs careful attention and should be addressed effectively.

Chairman TOM DAVIS. It has been a tough issue in the Congress. The House and Senate are a little divided on it as well.

Finally, the administration's proposal gives the President permanent funding authority for research, development and production of biochemical countermeasures. What do you think this could end up costing at the end of the day?

Dr. FAUCI. The initial projection that was made based—and again, this is something we try to scope out because you are dealing with scientific opportunities that can change due to breakthroughs as well as change in the risk assessment, but in the President's proposal, the 10-year proposal for the Project BioShield procurement was about $5.6 billion over 10 years.

Chairman TOM DAVIS. Our problem, of course, is we don't know what diseases could come forward.

Dr. FAUCI. It could be more, it could be less.

Dr. MCCLELLAN. I would like to emphasize, though, that none of this money gets spent unless, No. 1, we make a determination that the countermeasure is needed and is truly valuable. We set the term for the contract. If we don't think a countermeasure is worth the cost, it is not going to get a contract, and we don't actually pay—we don't pay any significant amount unless that countermeasure actually gets delivered and does work.

Chairman TOM DAVIS. What's clear is that the current law does not afford us the flexibility that we need to encourage industry.

Dr. FAUCI. We can't give assurances to them, as I said in my opening statement. We can't tell them and say we want to get involved in this. We are willing to take risks even. We have people who come to us and say, we've reached a certain point, and now we need to go to the next step of building a new plant or investing another $100 million or so, but we are willing to take that risk, but we're not willing to take a risk of being successful in what we do and then finding out that no one wants to buy the product. So can you give us an assurance under current law given the vicissitudes of the appropriation process? We really can't give them firm assurances that if they deliver, as Dr. McClellan said, a licensable or licensed biomedical countermeasure, we can't give them the kind of assurances under the current situation that we would be able to do under Project BioShield.

Chairman TOM DAVIS. Any other questions over this side?

Mr. WAXMAN. Thank you, Mr. Chairman.

Let me ask about the streamline procurement acquisition procedures. There is a simplified acquisition authority here, and these authorities in the law were established for commercially available items such as office furniture and automobiles. And the idea is there is a developed market for these products, and the government can rely on market forces to keep the prices low. When the government is bidding for a special government service, however, there is no market that's available to keep costs low, and two basic safeguards have been developed; one, requirements for bidding and full and open competition and, when the contract is cost-based, the ability to inspect the contractors' books.

As I understand it, the procurement provisions waive or relax both of these standards. I am in favor of speeding up the procurement where there is a need, but at the same time how do we protect the taxpayers? If the contract is cost-based, how does the government know it is not being overcharged if it can't audit the contractors' books? Anyone want to respond?

Dr. FAUCI. I'll take just a brief shot at it.

We appreciate that concern, and there's obviously a lot of scrutiny in what we'll be doing, because we're acting in only special circumstances. But your point is very well taken, and we're very sensitive to it. The main concern that we have is that we do not slow down the procurement process to the point where it interferes with the responsibility for what we have. We are not dead set against relooking at that with you, and we, in fact, would be willing to work with you and the committee on that concern which you've expressed. But the critical, really bottom-line issue is that we really cannot slow down the process, and if we can figure out a way to get it to do that, we would be——

Mr. WAXMAN. I understand that, but we are changing the procurement law, and if the government doesn't have a market to drive the prices lower, and it is a cost-based reimbursement, and we don't have the ability to look at their books and know whether they're getting ripped off, that puts us in a position of being deep pockets. And I think we've got to evaluate that balance here to make sure we're protecting the taxpayers and not just the American public.

Dr. MCCLELLAN. And if I could add, the whole goal here is to create something like a market. You're right, there is no market that exists now, but the contracting authorities that BioShield would create would permit more than one firm to compete to get this countermeasure produced first. And again, we're paying for results primarily, not for just costs along the way. The simplified acquisition authorities have been shown to work pretty well in combination with antikickback laws and fraud laws and the like to prevent those kinds of concerns in many cases.

Mr. WAXMAN. It will be a while before there would be a market. If you're helping a company develop a product for which there's no availability at the present time, do we help them with money, and then we streamline the process for them, and they develop it, and we give them the patent, and they'll have exclusivity over that, and then we're buying it from them, and we want to be sure since there's no real competition we're protecting our taxpayers' money?

Dr. MCCLELLAN. I do think we can create some competition there by contracting with more than one company and giving a larger payment to the one that gets there first.

Chairman TOM DAVIS. Would the gentleman yield?

Mr. WAXMAN. On the antikickback, that's a protection, but as I understand it, the antikickback law is exempted under the proposal, so we wouldn't have that available to us if that's something that won't come into play.

Chairman TOM DAVIS. I think the gentleman raises an interesting point. On the other hand, for the most part we're going to give this on a results-oriented basis. If companies go out and do research, and they come up with basically a dry hole, they probably get nothing; is that correct?

Dr. MCCLELLAN. That's right.

Chairman TOM DAVIS. Unlike a lot of IT contracts where we end up buying information technologies and spend billions and sometimes get systems that don't work. At least it is results-oriented, which cuts down the fraud, waste and abuse that could come otherwise. But there is a question of balance, and it's how sophisticated are we on our side, and look forward to working with Mr. Waxman and others trying to find the right balance.

Mr. WAXMAN. Let me ask a question on this liability issue. I understand why we want to give liability protection to the manufacturers of these products, and it is very much on their minds if you want to give them all the incentives. But on the other hand, if we're going to indemnify the companies that manufacture countermeasures by providing the liability protection, some of these products still may harm consumers. If the administration can guarantee liability protection to manufacturers, should it also compensate those who are injured by the products?

Dr. MCCLELLAN. There is a lot of discussion ongoing now about compensation in the case of smallpox, which is a countermeasure that does have some significant adverse effects in certain cases. The idea for the kinds of technologies that we hope to develop here is to have some that are significantly safer and more effective that would reduce the need for those kinds of compensation activities. And also the use here will be under conditions that are very much defined by the government in emergency situations and the like and that we at FDA approve and determine that treatments are appropriate for use under these circumstances. So it is a more limited case and problem. I know smallpox is on your mind, but it is a much more limited situation than that.

Mr. WAXMAN. Mr. Chairman, I want to take advantage of the fact that Dr. McClellan is here to ask him about a different issue unrelated to the BioShield. At a hearing——

Chairman TOM DAVIS. I am sure that wouldn't happen, but that's fine.

Mr. WAXMAN. If he doesn't feel ready to answer the question, I would certainly accept that response. But we had a hearing on Internet pharmacies, and a representative from the Federal Trade Commission testified that any claim that a dietary supplement containing ephedra is safe would be false and misleading under his view at the Federal Trade Commission. I want to know if you agreed with their view on the safety claims on ephedra products, and to ask you whether you are aware of any studies that prove that ephedra containing dietary supplements are safe for the general public.

Dr. MCCLELLAN. We just completed a review by the RAND Corp., that I know that you are familiar with because we talked with your staff about it, on the safety and effectiveness of ephedra. And as you know, under the dietary supplement law we don't get the evidence up front on dietary supplements if they are safe and effective before they go on the market. We have to prove a safety problem or an effectiveness problem before we can take any regulatory action, and that was the point of the RAND study.

Subsequent to the RAND study, we have reopened the record on FDA's old 1997 regulation to restrict use of ephedra based on safety and effectiveness concerns, and we have asked for comments from the public, and I noted today we just got one in from the American Heart Association, and I hope that there's going to be more coming before this comment period closes. That is going to help us address this issue of ephedra safety.

What the RAND report said, as you know, was that while there have been some serious adverse events associated with ephedra, they could not prove a causal link between ephedra use and those events.

Mr. WAXMAN. Let's flip it the other way. If you can't show that it's harmful, do you know of any studies that prove that ephedra-containing dietary supplements are safe?

Dr. MCCLELLAN. It hasn't been proven to be safe, but the statutory standard is not——

Mr. WAXMAN. I am not asking about the statutory standard. I understand that is important. But what do you think about the comment by the representative of the Federal Trade Commission if there was a claim that the supplements that contained ephedra was safe, that this would be a false and misleading statement?

Dr. MCCLELLAN. It could well be a problem with truthful and not misleading standards, which do govern both FTC's advertising regulations and our labeling regulations. So that is a potential concern. My hope is we can do more to address the concerns that exist today about the way that ephedra is marketed, and that's the reason that we reopened this comment period and have laid out our preliminary view that the law doesn't require us to prove that ephedra is unsafe; rather we need to demonstrate that it presents an unreasonable risk to the public as it's currently marketed, and we hope that we'll get comments from you about how we can best address that as well.

Mr. WAXMAN. Thank you very much.

Chairman TOM DAVIS. Mr. Shays, any more questions?

Mr. SHAYS. Yes, I do.

Dr. Fauci, what is the relationship between NIH and DOD joint vaccine acquisition of the JVAP program?

Dr. FAUCI. Thank you for the question, Mr. Shays. The NIH has worked in the past with DOD and in some respects with the JVAP program, and we are now increasing our collaborations particularly with USAMRIID. The Joint Vaccine Acquisition Program, which was operational in 1998, was focusing more on the long-term development of products against biological warfare, and we at the NIH feel that it doesn't directly address the urgent and civilian needs and demands that we have. And that's one of the reasons why we've looked for alternative ways to hasten the development and interest in industry in vaccine development. Although we've interacted with them on JVAP, but even more intensively, broadly with USAMRIID, this is not an important part of our program.

Mr. SHAYS. So your basic position is it's not going to fit into the Project BioShield program.

Dr. FAUCI. No, it's not in our minds, sir.

Mr. SHAYS. Has the JVAP been the subject of third-party evaluations?

Dr. FAUCI. Yes, it has. In December 2000, there was a report called the Top Report, a report to the Deputy Secretary of Defense by an independent panel of experts, and they came up with some areas that were problematic with regard to JVAP and talking about ways that need to be improving it. And I think instability of funding was cited as a major deficiency as well as some lack of scientific oversight. So it has been somewhat of a problem. I haven't——

Mr. SHAYS. Are you being a little gentle in describing the evaluations? There is $300 million that's been spent? I mean, weren't the reviews pretty strongly critical?

Dr. FAUCI. They were quite critical of the program, yes.

Mr. SHAYS. Dr. Klein, how would you kind of respond—first off, Dr. Fauci, is there anything you want to say about this program? You are basically telling me you're not going to—you don't see being involved in the BioShield program. Are there lessons we have learned from this in terms of what we do with BioShield?

Dr. FAUCI. I think so. We learned a lot of lessons along the way. One of the things I think we've learned that we have to have is we have built into BioShield a significant amount of scientific oversight and stability of funding and some strategic planning of where you are going to go and to try to bring in the very best of industry and not give them the full component, as Dr. McClellan has mentioned, until we have a deliverable product.

One of the difficulties with putting a lot of money up front and up forward without getting a guarantee of a product is that there is always the risk of failure, and that's what we're trying to avoid by making the stipulation of BioShield that you have to have a licensable product that's delivered before you get your full payment.

Mr. SHAYS. Dr. Klein, is there anything you want us to know about JVAP?

Dr. KLEIN. Congressman Shays, I think the comments made earlier are quite accurate. As you know, this program was started in about 1997. It's a 10-year program. So it was a start. But I think our experience with JVAP demonstrates BioShield's value; for example, incentives for companies to go toward making products. And then the other one I think is more important, certainly after September 11th, is that the interagency cooperation between DOD, DHHS and Homeland Security.

So I think we really need to look at this in a more comprehensive manner. As you know, JVAP was intended to meet the needs of the men and women in uniform. That was its initial intent. After September 11th I think we realized they are not the only ones that need these vaccines.

Mr. SHAYS. So far the program has spent a lot of money, and it has been found wanting, correct?

Dr. KLEIN. The original JVAP, the intent was good, but it has not been as successful as we wanted.

Mr. SHAYS. Let me just ask, Dr. Fauci, if we manage to engage the industry, what is the most useful role for NIH and its grantees? How does it focus on research that is not competitive and duplicative with that of the industry?

Dr. FAUCI. Traditionally, and we hope it continues and amplifies, that the NIH research has really been the fuel that fires the engine toward the ultimate translation into products, which the industry does so well. That is not to say that the industry does not do some very important research themselves, but it has really been essentially a continuum where NIH grantees provide the basic research, the proof of concept, and even the development up to, but not including, advanced development. We generally push the envelope into phase 1/phase 2 trials and the early part of development. That would be a natural marriage that we would see work well with BioShield to then call upon industry to make the investment, and what they do so well is delivering a product. So it's quite complementary, sir.

Mr. SHAYS. Mr. Chairman, may I ask one more question?

Mr. Brown, what are the problems the government faces in trying to engage biotech and pharmaceutical companies in launching research and development projects to develop medical countermeasures?

Mr. BROWN. I think it's the lack of a secure source of funding. They need to know that if we make the determination that there is an imminent danger and real threat out there, and they can produce what is results-oriented, they can show us a product, they're going to get paid for it. It is the lack of incentive.

Mr. SHAYS. Thank you.

Thank you, Mr. Chairman.

Chairman TOM DAVIS. Thank you all very much. We appreciate it very much and thank you for being here. It has been very, very helpful, and we are ready to move to our next panel of witnesses.

Our second panel includes industry and academic experts who will give us their views on this proposal. We have Frank Rapoport an attorney representing Aventis Pasteur. Next we will hear from Dr. Michael Friedman on behalf of the Pharmaceutical Research and Manufacturers Association of America. We also have Dr. Una Ryan, president of the AVANT Immuno-therapeutics located in Needham, MA. And Dr. Katherine Bowdish. She is president of the Alexion Antibody Technologies located in Cheshire, CT. And rounding out the panel is Dr. John Edwards, chief of infectious diseases at UCLA.

Give everyone a minute to make sure we have your name tags appropriately, and thank you for bearing with us through the questioning of the first panel.

We have a light in front, and it will be green for 4 minutes, and then it turns orange for the last minute. When it turns red, we want you to sum up. Your entire testimony is in the record, and we and our staff have read it all and have questions prepared on that, but you can use your 5 minutes to highlight.

I'm going to ask you to stand with me to be sworn in.

[Witnesses sworn.]

Chairman TOM DAVIS. We will start with Mr. Rapoport and move straight down the line.

STATEMENTS OF FRANK RAPOPORT, ATTORNEY AT LAW, MCKENNA LONG & ALDRIDGE, ON BEHALF OF AVENTIS PASTEUR; MICHAEL FRIEDMAN, CHIEF MEDICAL OFFICER FOR BIOMEDICAL PREPAREDNESS, PHARMACEUTICAL RESEARCH AND MANUFACTURERS OF AMERICA; UNA RYAN, PRESIDENT, AVANT IMMUNOTHERAPEUTICS, INC., NEEDHAM, MA; KATHERINE BOWDISH, Ph.D., PRESIDENT, ALEXION ANTIBODY TECHNOLOGIES, CHESHIRE, CT; AND JOHN EDWARDS, CHIEF OF INFECTIOUS DISEASES, HARBOR-UCLA MEDICAL CENTER, ON BEHALF OF THE INFECTIOUS DISEASES SOCIETY OF AMERICA

Mr. RAPOPORT. Good morning, Mr. Chairman and members of the committee. I am Frank Rapoport, a partner in the Philadelphia office of McKenna Long & Aldridge, where I practice government contract and public health law. I had the privilege of working both in the Reagan and Carter Justice Departments in the Government Contracts Section and more recently was involved in both smallpox procurements, the first one pre-September 11th, and the anthrax procurement more recently at NIH on behalf of Aventis Pasteur, the largest vaccine manufacturer in the world devoted entirely to vaccine research, development and manufacturing, manufacturing a billion and half doses annually, based in its headquarters in northeast Pennsylvania.

My purpose today is limited to offer some technical amendments to this bill which may make the difference between success and failure in either attracting the best and the brightest or simply those who have nothing to lose but accepting government money. I offer five points to achieve broader and bolder procurement authority, all giving discretion to the various Secretaries to use as arrows in their quiver.

There is no doubt that the existing government regulations, known affectionately as the FARS, give contracting officials ample authority to make contractors perform. Our five points today will protect the contractor against all but its own failure.

Point one, the bill, quite frankly, is a little stiff. It does not amply provide for a single procurement that combines both research and development and a guarantee of production. There must, in our view, be a linkage to get the attention of companies like Aventis, who are going to be passing up lost opportunities and feeling the uncertainty without commitment for production.

Point two is related to this. These contracts should also recognize the costs of capital and return on capital. It should assure payments sufficient to amortize investment, which would include return of capital and return on capital. The point is if we're not going to be accepting government money under R&D within this contract, we need to make sure that our investors feel comfortable that there is a product at the end of the pipeline and in the event, most importantly, of an early termination for convenience because, for instance, Dr. Fauci has found yet a better drug. The company must know that it's going to get reimbursed for the work that it spent under its own nickel under that government contract. The existing termination for convenience regulations do not allow for recovery of what we would call loss of interest or investor cost.

So when I suggest the bill is a little stiff, we feel it's a very good bill, but you need to be heard loud and clear that we want to give much broader authority to the Secretary to encourage companies to perform. How can this be accomplished in one contract vehicle? It would be one contract where research and development is included. We're not suggesting who's going to pay for that. That's up to the government to negotiate with the company. At the same time, there's a guarantee of production, but the cost of the units will not be determined until the research and development is over. This is always done in a privatized procurement. We call it price determination. That can be done to include the estimated costs of production as well as a capital charge.

Point three, we strongly encourage to move beyond plain vanilla government contracts, something you're well aware of which this committee called "other transactions" and is used routinely by DARPA and NASA and actually generated the Predator, the unmanned vehicle that is being used in Afghanistan. These are commercial-like arrangements that entice and allow government contractors like Aventis to feel free that they will get to protect their rights.

Point four as proposed in the bill, a 5-year contract without subsequent guaranteed appropriations appears to run afoul of 31 U.S.C. 1341. You certainly can take a minor correction to make sure that this act is taken care of.

Finally, the issue that you've heard already today, indemnity. We truly understand the urgency of this bill, but we feel obligated to note the issue of liability protection remains a concern for us. Both HHS and DHS have authority under Public Law 85–804. It has been used rarely. Most recently President Bush signed an Executive order which even cuts back on the authority of Public Law 85–804. Currently, while HHS has used this act, we understand it is not until after a contract is awarded. Imagine a bidder looking at dealing with inhalation airborne anthrax, doing clinical studies. A bidder company such as Aventis would like to know for its shareholders that it can bank on likelihood of indemnity postaward.

In summary, Mr. Chairman, thank you for the opportunity to testify on this important issue. As you know, we were the donor of 85 million doses of smallpox vaccine. We will be committed to supporting the efforts of the Secretaries to contributing to our common defense. Thank you again.

Chairman TOM DAVIS. Thank you very much.

[The prepared statement of Mr. Rapoport follows:]

McKenna Long & Aldridge LLP
Attorneys at Law

Aventis Pasteur Aventis

FRANK M. RAPOPORT, ESQUIRE
PARTNER, MCKENNA LONG & ALDRIDGE LLP
WASHINGTON, D.C.

TESTIFYING ON BEHALF OF
AVENTIS PASTEUR

BEFORE THE HOUSE GOVERNMENT REFORM COMMITTEE

REGARDING PROJECT BIOSHIELD ACT OF 2003

APRIL 4, 2003

Mr. Chairman and Members of the Committee, it is an honor for me to testify before you today regarding Project BioShield and its likely impact in bringing private sector talent and investment into our nation's BioDefense effort. I would also like to recognize Dr. Anthony Fauci and Dr. Mark McClellan for their testimony here today and their continued leadership on issues relating to the health of the American public. In addition, I would like to recognize the commitment and leadership on the issue of BioDefense that both the Department of Defense, as evidenced by Dr. Dale Klein's participation in this hearing, and the Department of Homeland Security, represented today by Mr. Michael Brown, have shown in leading the Nation's war on terrorism. Finally, Mr. Chairman, I applaud your immediate consideration of the proposed Project BioShield initiative and the leadership you and this committee have shown in the area of Federal procurement policy and national security.

I appear before you today representing one company – Aventis Pasteur. Aventis Pasteur is the largest company in the world devoted entirely to vaccine research, development, and manufacturing. Aventis Pasteur produces approximately 1.4 billion doses of vaccines annually, making it possible to protect 500 million people across the globe. The company offers the broadest range of vaccines, providing protection against 20 bacterial and viral diseases.

The company manufactures influenza vaccine and several other vaccines at its United States headquarters in Swiftwater, Pennsylvania. Over the years, Aventis Pasteur has had enormous successes, including the first application of conjugate vaccine technology and the licensing of the first infant acellular pertussis vaccine. While being involved in vaccine development, Aventis Pasteur also routinely supplies vaccines and biologicals needed by both civilian and military populations, including vaccines against tetanus and diphtheria, yellow fever, Japanese encephalitis, meningitis, typhoid fever, and influenza to name a few.

Aventis Pasteur has partnered with the Federal government in times of peace as well as in times of conflict. Immediately following the attacks on the World Trade Center on September 11, 2001, Aventis Pasteur worked closely with metropolitan New York and New Jersey public health and city officials to donate 50,000 doses of Tetanus Diphtheria Toxoids Adsorbed vaccine to the relief efforts. Most recently in 2002, Aventis Pasteur demonstrated this commitment by donating approximately 85 million doses of smallpox vaccine to the Federal government's emergency preparedness stockpiles. The company has always supplied the United States military with needed vaccines, including those being used today by our troops fighting in Iraq. The company has responded to more than one Federal request for proposal for BioDefense measures, and therefore, has current experience on this subject. Finally, Aventis Pasteur has been a leading participant in the Global Polio Eradication Initiative, a partnership created to deliver polio vaccine to every child under five, worldwide. Aventis Pasteur has donated a total of 120 million vaccine doses since 1997 under this initiative.

Aventis Pasteur supports the objectives of Project BioShield to expedite the Federal government's ability to contract for needed BioDefense products and to provide important certainty to applicants that money will be available to meet contractual commitments over a period of years. Development and production of complex medical and biological products requires a number of years under the most favorable circumstances and multi-year contracting needs to be available. The legislation, as proposed, is a significant step forward in preparing the Nation to meet the challenge of defending against bio-terror. There is no more critical time than now for this undertaking.

We recognize that the proposed legislation includes provisions of importance to the Administration. However, Congress can seize the opportunity to also make minor, but significant, changes to the bill to eliminate or ease frictions and constraints in current contracting procedures as they relate to the complicated development and manufacture of BioDefense products. These changes will dramatically strengthen Project BioShield and help ensure that its most important objective -- to ensure the efficient development of needed safe and effective BioDefense products -- is achieved.

Our proposed changes are as follows:

Provide for enough time to allow for R&D and production

The proposed legislation provides the authority to enter into "contracts" for a period not to exceed five years, but does not specifically address the implications of 31 U.S.C. §§ 1341 and 1342 (commonly called the "Anti-Deficiency Act"). Thus, Aventis Pasteur suggests language be included in the proposed legislation that makes clear that this authority is notwithstanding any restrictions placed on such agreements by the Anti-Deficiency Act or any other provision of law. This change is necessary regardless of the fact that the proposed legislation anticipates funding to be drawn from unobligated Treasury funds.

We are advised that an effective approach to addressing multi-year funding is to allow for the use of moneys in the Treasury not otherwise obligated. Aventis

Pasteur supports this "permanent, indefinite appropriation authority" approach as an improvement to the current contracting system for medical products. We understand this requires Congress to modify its usual approach to appropriations. However, these are unusual times requiring flexibility in this unique area of procurement. We assume checks and balances are in place to ensure appropriate stewardship and the use of this approach can be developed to protect the taxpayers' money. However, it is this concept which can provide the reliability, not currently present, that the money will be available to take the product through research, development and manufacturing. Finally, this type of authority already exists in some DoD programs used to develop cutting edge weapons systems.

In order to achieve the intended goal of creating a market for BioDefense vaccines and countermeasures, and satisfying the demand for these items through private, rather than public supply channels, private industry simply must be assured that the government market will be in place for some reasonable period of time before it commits the massive resources necessary (e.g., people, equipment, facilities, etc.) to meet the demands of the newly created market. Without such assurance, it will be all but impossible to generate interest from investors or lenders to allow for purely speculative (and truly enormous) capital expenditures. In addition, the lost opportunity costs to a company that pursues the Federal market in lieu of producing commercial products would be staggering if the Federal market never materializes due to a lack of funding. There is simply no other way to accomplish the goal using private sector resources without an assurance that the Federal government will have the financial resources necessary to make these purchases.

Provide for express authority to enter into a single agreement for research, development and production

We support strongly the need to provide for the possibility of the Federal government entering into agreements (including contracts, grants, cooperative agreements, and "other transactions") that permit a BioDefense contractor to engage in research and development with the assurance of production under a single agreement. While this appears to be the intention of the legislation, the proposed legislation does not make this authority clear. A company like Aventis Pasteur, which not only does research and development, but emphasizes the reliable manufacture of millions of doses of vaccines, needs the certainty that satisfactory completion of research and development will lead to a manufacturing agreement.

We are not recommending that Congress mandate the precise nature of such agreements. However, the Secretary should be expressly given the maximum amount of flexibility possible to negotiate the best deal for the Federal government. To that end, the Secretary should be expressly provided with the ability to enter into agreements that "guarantee production" on a fixed-price, cost reimbursement, or combination thereof, basis where appropriate.

Aventis Pasteur suggests language be included in the proposed legislation to make clear that the Secretary of Health and Human Services has the authority to enter into such agreements.

Provide for express authority to enter into agreements other than contracts

The proposed legislation suggests that the Secretary of Health and Human Services is to be provided the authority to enter into "agreements" and other "acquisition instruments" but that such agreements are not to be limited to simply "contracts." While this appears to be the intention of the legislation, the proposed legislation does not make this authority to enter into "other transactions" clear.

Aventis Pasteur suggests language be included in the proposed legislation to make clear that authority is provided to the Secretary to enter into agreements and other acquisition instruments that include contracts, grants, cooperative agreements, and "other transactions" in order to provide the maximum degree of flexibility suggested by the proposed legislation. "Other transaction" authority will permit agreements between HHS and industry that more closely resemble a fully negotiated commercial transaction. Similar authority has been provided to both the Department of Defense and NASA and has resulted in numerous success stories including, most recently, the "Predator" program in use in Afghanistan today.

Provide for the authority to ensure that the price of any product sold to the government may reflect the costs of private financing and that these costs are reflected in any termination settlement

It is our experience that in order to stimulate private investment in BioDefense countermeasure research, development, and production, private investors must be assured that they have the potential to receive a return on their investment, both in the pricing of the end product and in the event the government elects to terminate the agreement for its convenience. The proposed legislation does not account for the implications of using private investment to finance research, development, and production of biomedical countermeasures.

Aventis Pasteur suggests language be included in the proposed legislation that permits the Secretary of Health and Human Services to enter into agreements that allow the end price of any biomedical countermeasure to reflect the cost of private financing, including costs of capital and return on equity investment.

In addition, under current Federal Acquisition Regulations (FAR), when a contract is terminated for the convenience of the government, contractors may recover their costs of performance through the date of termination plus a reasonable profit on those costs in addition to settlement expenses associated with ceasing performance, negotiating termination liability, and disposing of equipment and materials. The terms vary slightly, depending upon the specific language of the specific "termination for convenience" clause used in the contract. However, one of the costs the FAR expressly prohibits -- and one which very likely will apply to Project BioShield contracts -- is capital financing costs.

Specifically, the program envisioned by the proposed legislation likely will be awarded via competitive negotiations. In such instances, the agency (here, HHS) negotiates proposals with one or more contractors. In such cases, the FAR expressly prohibits contractors from recovering as part of their contract price interest on borrowings (however represented) as well as costs of financing and refinancing capital. *See* FAR 31.205-20. Therefore, to recover return on equity costs and other capital financing arrangements, the existing regulations must be changed.

In order to facilitate this change, Aventis Pasteur suggests language be included in the proposed legislation that requires the Secretary of Health and Human Services to include within an agreement a termination clause that requires the costs of capital and return on equity to be included in any settlement in the event the government terminates the agreement for convenience.

Provide for the authority to indemnify and/or limit the extent of liability for any contractor engaging in research, development, and production of BioDefense countermeasures

The issue of the potential liability for any entity that provides, or performs research and development related to, BioDefense countermeasures absolutely must be addressed in order to stimulate private sector interest in entering into agreements for such countermeasures. Our experience was that the absence of liability protection was a major obstacle in the recent procurement by NIH for development of the next-generation Anthrax vaccine and continues to be a major hurdle for our company. We would try to obtain commercial insurance, but the practical reality today is that it is unlikely to be available for these projects given their nature. The proposed legislation is silent with respect to addressing liability. We appreciate the need for urgency in passing Project BioShield, but at the same time, we feel obligated to note that the issue of liability protection remains a concern for Aventis Pasteur.

Both the Secretary of Health and Human Services and the Secretary of Homeland Security currently have the authority to provide for Federal indemnity to private entities engaging in research, development, and production of biomedical countermeasures under Public Law 85-804. However, use of such authority is extremely rare. It is important to note that President Bush recently revised Executive Order 10,789 governing use of the authority to provide for indemnity under Public Law 85-804. We are curious to see how this evolution of policy will not severely limit the ability of the Secretaries of Health and Human Services and Homeland Security to exercise this authority.

Finally, while HHS is currently using its authority under Public Law 85-804 in very limited circumstances, it is our best understanding that the agency is not providing indemnity until a contact is awarded – and will not guarantee that indemnity is forthcoming as part of the award process. Aventis Pasteur urges Congress and the Administration to ensure that such indemnification is provided where appropriate.

Mr. Chairman, thank you for the opportunity to testify on this tremendously important issue. Aventis Pasteur has been an remains committed to contributing to our nation's common defense. I will be pleased to respond to any questions from members of the Committee.

Chairman TOM DAVIS. Dr. Friedman.

Dr. FRIEDMAN. Thank you, Mr. Chairman and distinguished Members. On behalf of the Pharmaceutical Research and Manufacturers of America, I am pleased to be here today to share with you the views of the research-based pharmaceutical industry and the President's Project BioShield Initiative.

Biological weapons represent an increasingly serious danger to people around the world. The dynamic complexity of the problem is demonstrated by science's difficulties in dealing with naturally occurring infectious disease as well as intentional bioterrorist threats. While PhRMA companies are developing more than 200 new medicines to treat or prevent various infectious diseases, reports by the National Academy of Sciences, the NIH Blue Ribbon Panel for Biodefense Research, and the U.S. Defense Science Board make it clear that an even larger number of more diverse types of countermeasures must be developed, and they must be developed promptly.

Although the basic science research required for countermeasure development is being supported by Federal agencies, it is widely recognized that more sponsored research is needed. There also needs to be more flexible authority and more resources for regulatory agencies; in short, those things which will advance the development and production of the countermeasures.

PhRMA member companies have been active in moving forward on countermeasure research and development. As indicated in my written testimony, for example, PhRMA is working with CDC, DOD, NIH, FDA and academia to support invitro studies of five important pathogens as model systems for antibiotic testing. Several companies are working with the National Institutes of Allergy and Infectious Diseases to help test existing antibiotics against plague. Other examples of ongoing collaboration are outlined in my testimony.

A cooperative and collaborative research and development effort which engages industry, government and academia will, however, be essential to this effort. PhRMA believes that Project BioShield is an important step toward this, and we support the three main components of the President's proposal.

The President's proposal speaks primarily to the early and to the later stages and the lengthy high risk and costly process of bringing new medicines to the market. It does not, however, speak to the time-consuming and resource-intensive middle portion of that process, which is largely our responsibility. Further, research into biothreat countermeasures presents challenges beyond those ordinarily encountered in nonbiodefense R&D. These include scientific challenges, economic challenges and legal challenges, and I will enumerate a couple, if I may.

For example, some products will be distributed without the typical battery of clinical trials that are required for FDA approval. All medicines present inherent and unavoidable risk of adverse events. As a result manufacturers may be exposed to devastating product liability suits. Private insurance can be unavailable or prohibitively expensive.

Second, the need for rapid development of countermeasures may require the sharing of scientific information and cooperation among companies; for example, the sharing of data by researchers working in different laboratories. Collaboration and cooperation in this research might create exposure under current antitrust laws.

Third, diverting resources from research and development of other medicines will affect the future availability of treatments and cures for patients with other serious health conditions, especially since only a tiny percent of all drugs that enter testing ever demonstrate sufficient human safety and acceptable efficacy.

The allocation of resources can be particularly difficult with few products in the pipeline. In order to best meet the public health needs of our citizens, PhRMA looks forward to working with in, a transparent manner, Congress and the administration to enact measures that will provide appropriate product liability protection for products that are procured under BioShield and for products that are distributed under the emergency authorization procedures of BioShield. Although existing indemnification authorities are a helpful step in the right direction for some government contractors, they are not an appropriate model for legislation implementing Project BioShield. Instead, we would urge Congress and the administration to expand and, as appropriate, modify the liability protection model that this Congress has already put in place for smallpox.

PhRMA also looks forward to working closely with Congress and the administration to enact narrowly tailored measures to address existing antitrust constraints as appropriate in order to allow needed collaboration and consortium among scientists and industries. My written testimony includes the memorandum from outside counsel explaining both the need and the precedent for a narrowly tailored antitrust provision that would apply in this very special context.

Cooperation and strong commitment from all parties will be necessary in the months and years to come as our Nation seeks to protect itself against the terrible threats of biowarfare and bioterrorism. America's pharmaceutical companies look forward to doing our part. I thank you for this opportunity to address you and look forward to answering your questions. Thank you.

Chairman TOM DAVIS. Thank you very much.

[The prepared statement of Dr. Friedman follows:]

Statement PhRMA

DR. MICHAEL A. FRIEDMAN

FOR THE

PHARMACEUTICAL RESEARCH AND MANUFACTURERS OF AMERICA

BEFORE THE

COMMITTEE ON GOVERNMENT REFORM

April 4, 2003

The Pharmaceutical Research and Manufacturers of America (PhRMA) appreciates the opportunity to share with the Committee the views of the research-based pharmaceutical industry on the President's Project Bioshield Initiative. PhRMA represents the country's leading research-based pharmaceutical and biotechnology companies, which invested an estimated $32 billion in 2002 in developing new medicines to help and heal patients.

PhRMA member companies join others who are convinced that biological weapons present a serious and increasing danger to people around the world. The pharmaceutical industry is dedicated to the development of innovative therapies and vaccines to counter unmet medical needs. Because a substantial proportion of the unmet medical need in the United States and worldwide is both directly and indirectly related to infectious diseases, we understand only too well the seriousness of the threat of biological agents if used as weapons of war.

The complexity of the problem of biological weapons is best demonstrated by humanity's ongoing difficulty in dealing with infectious agents as the cause of natural disease, let alone their potential use for intentional concentrated exposure of selected populations. The threat represented by infectious diseases – such as HIV, malaria, and tuberculosis – is real and all too well demonstrated by the deaths of over 5 million people annually from these three diseases alone. All together, infectious diseases claim more than 100,000 American lives each year, and cost more than $30 billion annually in direct treatment expenses alone. At last count, PhRMA member companies were developing 256 new medicines to treat or prevent infectious diseases; medicines which include brand new classes of antibiotics, new vaccines (including edible vaccines), antifungals, antivirals, and immune enhancers.

Reports from the National Academy of Sciences, the NIH Blue Ribbon Panel for Biodefense Research, and the US Defense Science Board, make clear that a large number of countermeasures to biothreats must also be developed. These countermeasures include vaccines, therapeutics, and diagnostics. The basic science research required for countermeasure development has already been stimulated by funds appropriated to various federal agencies including the Department of Health and Human Services and the Department of Defense. However it is widely recognized that more is needed with respect to funding of basic research, to increased authority for funding and regulatory agencies, and to the advanced development and production of the countermeasures.

A cooperative and collaborative research and development effort, which engages industry, government, and academia, will be essential to that effort. Existing medicines are not sufficient to combat the biological weapons already developed. Research and development into new medicines is a lengthy, risky, and expensive endeavor. Research into biothreat countermeasures involves several challenges above and beyond those encountered in non-biodefense R&D. For example, biodefense R&D requires working with dangerous pathogens in highly specialized facilities, and developing countermeasures without a full picture of the risk of disease (because we cannot see into the mind of the terrorist) or the benefit of the treatment (because there are often no patients with the disease, which prevents clinical testing for efficacy).

PhRMA and its member companies are already working closely with federal agencies and academia to move forward with this research. For example, PhRMA is working with CDC, DoD, NIH, FDA, and academia to support in vitro studies of five pathogens (B. anthracis, Y. pestis, Brucella spp., F. tularensis, and Burkholderia spp.) for testing of existing antibiotics. Several companies are working with the National Institute of Allergy and Infectious Diseases (NIAID), the Department of Defense, and the FDA to test existing antibiotics against plague, and PhRMA will cosponsor a workshop with interested parties to determine how best to expand labeling of other existing antibiotics that may be effective against the top biothreat agents. PhRMA committees continue to work with FDA to clarify and improve existing regulations that pertain to biothreat countermeasure research, such as Part 600 (the Spore Formers Rule, which imposes requirements on use of facilities or equipment that have been used with spore forming organisms), and the Animal Rule (which allows efficacy testing in animals where testing in humans would be impossible or unethical). We have prepared educational materials for the public on anthrax, smallpox, and vaccinia, and we are working on materials addressing tularemia and plague. Dr. Gail Cassell, PhRMA's Chief Scientific Officer for Emergency Preparedness and Vice President, Scientific Affairs at Eli Lilly & Co., sits on Secretary Thompson's Advisory Council on Public Health Preparedness. A Biosurveillance workgroup involving PhRMA and other private sector companies (TIGR, IBM, and Roche Diagnostics) along with federal agencies (CDC, DoD, NIH) and the World Health Organization to establish a global infectious disease electronic surveillance network.

PhRMA believes that Project Bioshield, announced by President Bush in his 2003 State of the Union address, is an important step forward in the effort to ensure the development of modern, effective medicines and vaccines against biothreats and to ensure that these medicines are made available in a timely and efficient manner. PhRMA generally supports the three main components of the President's proposal: first, the creation of a permanent indefinite funding authority to spur the development of medicines and vaccines by the private sector; second, new authority for NIH to speed promising R&D through streamlined hiring and procurement mechanisms and increased flexibility to award contracts and grants; and third, new FDA emergency use authorization for promising treatments still under development.

At the same time, however, it is necessary to recognize scientific, legal, and economic impediments to the research and development of biodefense products. Manufacturers may be exposed to devastating product-liability suits. Some of these would arise out of adverse events that are unavoidable given the nature of the products, and some could arise simply because the products were made available without the usual battery of clinical trials required for FDA-approved products. Private insurance can be unavailable or prohibitively expensive for such products. The decision to divert resources from the research and development of medicines for serious illnesses like heart disease can be financially risky, especially when a countermeasure may never be purchased or used, and especially for companies with few products in the pipeline. (Diverting resources from research and development of these other medicines will also affect the future availability of treatments and cures for patients with other serious health conditions — especially since less than ten percent of all drugs that enter testing ever demonstrate sufficient safety and acceptable efficacy.) The need for urgent development of medicines may require the sharing of information and cooperation among companies, which can raise antitrust concerns. The scientific challenges inherent in research into bioterrorism countermeasures, for example, may require cooperation and collaboration among scientific experts in different companies. (For example, there have been only two new classes of antibiotics developed in the last 40 years.) PhRMA looks

forward to working closely with Congress and the Administration to enact measures that will provide appropriate product liability protection and address these antitrust constraints.

Cooperation and strong commitment from all parties will be necessary in the months and years to come, as our nation seeks to protect itself against the terrible threats of biowarfare and bioterrorism. America's pharmaceutical companies look forward to doing our part.

We thank you for your time and look forward to answering your questions.

COVINGTON & BURLING

March 25, 2003

The Need for an Antitrust Exemption to Enable Pharmaceutical Companies to Respond to Government Requests for Help to Combat Bioterrorism

In the aftermath of the attacks of September 11 and the use of anthrax as a terror weapon, the pharmaceutical industry has been asked by various government officials, particularly the Secretary of Heath and Human Services, to help reduce our vulnerability to the threat of bioterrorism. The antitrust laws present a significant restraint on the pharmaceutical industry's ability to provide assistance. Accordingly, a limited antitrust exemption is warranted for joint efforts undertaken under government auspices to develop bioterrorism countermeasures. Such an exemption, for which there are several historical precedents, would further the government's program to ensure that the country is prepared to respond to an act of bioterrorism and would not undermine the important protections imposed by the antitrust laws.

Fighting Bioterrorism Will Require A Coordinated Industry Response

As the country learns more about the potential threats posed by bioterrorism, the research and production expertise of the nation's pharmaceutical industry could be called into service in a variety of ways. Likely requests for assistance include:

- An exchange of information by pharmaceutical companies on individual vaccine manufacturing capacity to develop an industry aggregate assessment of capacity.
- An HHS sponsored agreement that one group of pharmaceutical companies devote research and manufacturing capacity to one area, such as a smallpox vaccine, and that another group of companies focus on another area, such as anthrax treatments.
- An HHS request that the companies agree that, in the event of a bioterrorism event, they will dedicate their research and manufacturing resources on an emergency basis in a manner directed by HHS.
- A procedure by which pharmaceutical companies share research results and manufacturing best practices to allow for the rapid production of needed bioterrorism countermeasures.

While each of these steps would increase the nation's ability to respond to the bioterrorism threat, individual pharmaceutical companies may be unable to participate in these types of joint efforts without some assurance that its conduct will not be challenged as a violation of the antitrust laws.

The Antitrust Laws Bar Joint Action by Competitors Regardless of Social Need

Section 1 of the Sherman Act -- the provision of the antitrust laws most pertinent to this issue -- prohibits agreements between competitors that unreasonably restrain trade. The pharmaceutical companies would be hampered in their ability to defend joint responses to government requests notwithstanding the existence of an overwhelming public health benefit for several reasons:

- Some agreements, including agreements among competitors to allocate resources across a range of projects, can be *per se* illegal notwithstanding compelling justifications.

- Even under the rule of reason, the Supreme Court has held that agreements must be justified under the Sherman Act as promoting competition and may not be justified by public policy considerations, such as safety and health.

- Absent specific statutory authorization, government officials lack authority to grant immunity from antitrust challenge.

Furthermore, antitrust claims frequently are expensive to defend and inherently difficult to predict in their outcome. As a matter of prudent business practice, pharmaceutical companies, pursuant to written antitrust guidelines, routinely avoid any discussions with competitors that could give rise to a challenge under the antitrust laws. Thus, even some limited discussions that may not themselves constitute antitrust violations may be hindered due to the risk that such discussions will be taken out of context by an antitrust plaintiff.

Each of the agreements described above could potentially be challenged by a private plaintiff or a government entity as antitrust violations. The fact that they were undertaken at the request of the federal government to bolster the country's defenses to a bioterrorist attack or as part of an emergency response to a bioterrorism event does not remove them from the reach of the antitrust laws. Courts have squarely rejected as being "without merit" a claim by an antitrust defendant that "in the emergency of war, the war power of the Federal Government and military authorities takes precedence over the civil law and nullified the Sherman Act during the emergency."[1]

The Necessary Cooperation Cannot Occur Without A Specific Exemption

Opponents of a limited antitrust exemption for bioterrorism preparations typically question whether (*i*) the assistance requested by the government actually places the responding companies at risk of violating the antitrust laws or (*ii*) whether existing provisions for facilitating industry cooperative efforts may provide the necessary assurance. The answer to those questions are yes, an antitrust risk does exist, and no, existing procedures are not sufficient to remove that risk.

The first potential request for assistance described above relates to a government initiated survey of productive capacity. In theory, such information could be collected on a strictly bilateral basis by HHS and then only shared with industry, if at all, in an aggregated form. Trade associations routinely collect data in a similar fashion without violating the antitrust laws. The utility of such data, however, is limited because of the difficulty of comparing productive assets. HHS needs more than a series of historical production data from each company. To understand fully the industry's productive capacity, HHS needs to be able to compare each company's assets and assess how they might be used either alone or in conjunction with assets held by other companies in the fight against bioterrorism. Further, HHS needs to understand how existing assets dedicated to producing certain products could be expanded and/or converted to new uses. HHS cannot conduct such evaluations on its own. Rather, the companies may need to sit down together, under the auspices of HHS, to explore how they can each best contribute to the national defense.

Another area of potential cooperation that would raise antitrust issues includes discussions of which research areas should take priority for a given company. The antitrust laws expect that each company will assess the likely profitability of a given line of research and

---

[1] *United States v. General Inst. Corp.*, 87 F.Supp. 157, 163-4 (D.N.J. 1949).

individually plan its research focus accordingly. In the past, Congress has recognized that such an approach may not always result in the socially optimal result. For example, the legislation providing special incentives for the pharmaceutical industry to engage in research on "orphan drugs" for diseases that affect small numbers of people demonstrates that market incentives may not produce the drugs America needs. A similar situation exists here, although the problem is not the size of the potential market; a bioterrorism event could affect millions. Rather the problem is the, hopefully small, likelihood that such a market will ever develop and the possibility that companies may not pursue research on some of the threats. The pharmaceutical industry is willing to do the work to prepare for each threat identified by HHS, but it makes no sense for each company to attempt to pursue every area in which the government might request research. The antitrust laws would at least call into question, and likely prohibit, an agreement among the pharmaceutical manufacturers to allocate research efforts among potential threats or to suspend non-bioterrorism research projects if requested by HHS.

A third area of potential concern is the sharing of research results or production techniques to enable all participating manufacturers to take advantage of the latest technology. Such cooperation also may allow companies to avoid duplicating, possibly at government expense, unproductive efforts undertaken by other companies. In the normal commercial context, such process improvements are treated as competitively sensitive information and their sharing would raise a question as to whether impermissible collaboration is occurring. To obtain the most effective bioterrorism countermeasures possible, however, exactly that type of sharing may be required.

Existing Antitrust Procedures Regarding Joint Ventures Are Inadequate

The existing procedures designed to facilitate cooperative conduct under the antitrust laws would not provide adequate protection for the activities described in the preceding paragraphs. The National Cooperative Research & Production Act of 1993 ("NCRPA")[2] provides some protection for joint research projects, but does not provide actual immunity from

[2] 15 U.S.C. §§ 4301-05.

the antitrust laws.[3] Thus, companies may still be dragged into litigation by competitors or consumer groups seeking to second guess the government decision to draw on the industry's expertise.

Similar problems exist with a business review letter from the Antitrust Division of the Justice Department or an advisory opinion from the FTC. These procedures allow businesses to request a statement of the government's current enforcement intentions with respect to a proposed course of conduct. One notable shortcoming of this procedure is that it has no effect on the ability of private plaintiffs to bring suit. Furthermore, the Antitrust Division will only provide a business review letter for proposed, not on-going, conduct. The nation's anti-bioterrorism preparations could be held up while the Justice Department bureaucracy ruminates over the industry request. Finally, even if a favorable letter is issued, it constitutes no more than a statement of present intent; no immunity is conferred. The FTC advisory opinion process presents the same problems. The limited comfort offered by a business review letter or an advisory letter is simply not sufficient for companies to suspend their normal antitrust guidelines and participate in activities that could entangle them in costly investigations or litigation.

History Offers Numerous Precedents for a Limited Antitrust Exemption

The Supreme Court has repeatedly said that "[t]he Sherman Act reflects a legislative judgment that *ultimately* competition will produce not only lower prices, but also better goods and services."[4] In a time of national emergency, there may not be the time to allow for the competitive process to produce the mix of goods and services society needs. Accordingly, there is a long history of providing legislative exemptions from the antitrust laws in specific areas. For example, during World War II, the War Production Board, the entity that was responsible for coordinating the mobilization of the U.S. economy for war production, had authority to

---

[3] A NCRPA filing limits the liability of the joint venture participants to actual (rather than treble) damages in certain circumstances and allows for the recovery of attorney fees by any defendants that prevail in actions found to be "frivolous, unreasonable, without foundation, or bad faith."

[4] *National Society of Professional Engineers v. United States*, 435 U.S. 679, 695 (1978) (emphasis added).

> certify to the Attorney General in writing that the doing of any act or thing, or the omission to do any act or thing, by one or more persons . . . is requisite to the prosecution of the war, [and] such act, thing or omission shall be deemed in the public interest and no prosecution or civil action shall be commenced with reference thereto under the antitrust laws of the United States or the Federal Trade Commission Act.[5]

During World War II, this provision was invoked in a number of areas, including the efficient production of railroad freight cars, conservation programs in the dairy industry, and the pooling of information regarding the manufacture of Lucite, a newly developed plastic important to the war effort.[6]

The War Production Board's power to grant exemptions from the antitrust laws was designed to alleviate industry concerns that they would incur antitrust liability from responding to government requests for assistance. In the 1930s, the major oil companies had become ensnared in antitrust litigation arising from their participation in cooperative ventures established by the National Industrial Recovery Act as a means of stabilizing the industry.[7] Faced with a recent example of how participating in government sponsored programs could result in antitrust problems, both industry and government leaders sought a way to ensure full and effective participation by industry.

Perhaps the most pertinent example of an antitrust exemption granted for wartime needs concerns the development of penicillin. Penicillin had been discovered in 1928 by Alexander Fleming, but had not been put into widespread clinical use. One major problem was devising an

---

[5] 56 Stat. 351 § 12. The Attorney General was required to give public notice when a certificate was issued and report to Congress periodically on exemptions granted by the WPB under this provision, but the WPB procedure for initially invoking the exemption was designed for flexible and speedy implementation.

[6] *See* Harold L. Schilz, *Voluntary Industry Agreements and Their Exemption From the Antitrust Laws*, 40 VIRGINIA L. REV. 1, 4 (1954).

[7] *See United States v. Socony-Vacuum Oil Co.*, 310 U.S. 150, 170-77 (1940); Schilz, *supra*, at 2-3.

appropriate manufacturing process for large-scale production. The War Production Board invoked the antitrust immunity provision quoted above to allow for the exchange of technical information regarding penicillin production among the various pharmaceutical firms participating in the program. A history of the penicillin program written by a scientist involved in the effort notes that "the free exchange of information made possible by the lifting of the U.S. antitrust law controls undoubtedly sped mass production during 1944-45" and that it may have even "led to increased competition among firms that might not otherwise have undertaken to manufacture the drug commercially."[8]

Congress has also granted antitrust immunity in areas not involving national security where there was a perceived need for joint industry action. The Television Program Improvement Act of 1990 created a three-year exemption from the antitrust laws for the purpose of "developing and disseminating voluntary guidelines designed to alleviate the negative impact of violence in telecast material."[9] Specific legislative exemptions also exist for associations formed solely to engage in export trade (Webb-Pomerene Act, 15 U.S.C. §§ 61-66), agricultural cooperatives (Capper-Volstead Act, 7 U.S.C. §§ 291-292), and negotiations between sports leagues and television broadcasters (Sports Broadcasting Act, 15 U.S.C. §§ 1291-1295).

One further existing statutory immunity provision merits mention. The Defense Production Act of 1950 allows the President, or his designee, to "consult with representatives of industry . . . and other interests in order to provide for the making by such persons, with the approval of the President, of voluntary agreements and plans of action to help provide for the defense of the United States . . . ." 50 U.S.C. App. § 2158(c)(1). Voluntary agreements formed under the aegis of the Defense Production Act are exempt from the antitrust laws assuming certain procedural provisions are followed. The Defense Production Act has typically been used for the production of military equipment, such as ammunition and armored vehicles.

---

[8] Gladys Hoby, PENICILLIN: MEETING THE CHALLENGE (Yale Univ. Press, 1985) at 213.

[9] Pub. L. No. 101-650 § 501, 104 Stat. 5127 (1990)

While a useful example of the need for antitrust exemptions in this general area, the Defense Production Act does not adequately address the government's likely needs in the bioterrorism context. With respect to manufacturing efforts, the scope of the Act appears to be limited to "the expansion of productive capacity and supply beyond levels needed to meet essential civilian demand." Many of the bioterrorism countermeasures contemplated would be for civilian, not exclusively military, use. The Defense Production Act includes extensive disclosure provisions that may deter companies from sharing confidential information and that may not adequately protect national security interests. The Defense Production Act also contains detailed procedural provisions, including preapproval requirements even for consultations, that may prove too burdensome and that may cause intolerable delays in the bioterrorism context.

The Proposed Exemption is Narrowly Focused and Provides for Appropriate Oversight

Under the proposed exemption, entities may engage in joint action related to anti-bioterrorism activities "for the purpose of, and limited to, assuring or expediting the development, production, distribution, or sale of [bioterrorism] countermeasures" without incurring any liability under the federal or state antitrust laws. The antitrust exemption extends no further than the specific cooperation necessary to respond to the threat of bioterrorism and specifically excludes "exchanging information among competitors relating to costs, sales, profitability, prices, marketing, or distribution" where such information "is not reasonably necessary to carry out the purposes of covered bio-terrorism activities."

The exemption requires the participating parties to file notifications of their joint activity with the Antitrust Division of the Department of Justice, the Federal Trade Commission, and the Secretary of HHS. The Attorney General, after taking into consideration the views of the FTC and HHS, can nullify the antitrust exemption in a specific instance by determining that exempting the joint action described in the notification would not further the public interest. The Attorney General must also provide public notice of the identity of the participants to an agreement exempted under this provision and the agreement's area of planned activity. This provision provides a second check on any possible anticompetitive activities growing out of cooperative ventures authorized by the Act.

Chairman TOM DAVIS. Dr. Ryan.

Ms. RYAN. Mr. Chairman and members of the committee, thank you very much for inviting me to testify before you on Project BioShield. I am the president and CEO of AVANT Immunotherapeutics, a small 60-person biotech company in Massachusetts. I am also on the board of the Biotechnology Industry Organization, and I am chairman-elect of the Massachusetts Biotechnology Council.

As the Federal Government embarks on BioShield, a new and challenging program to fight bioterrorism and biological warfare, let me assure you that the biotechnology industry stands ready to contribute and work toward its success. Our eagerness to participate, however, cannot be unqualified. As the leader of a small company, I cannot embark on the development and supply of biodefense vaccines if doing so doesn't make business sense.

Let me, if I may, give you my view of BioShield from the perspective of a small company. AVANT is a small company, and it's a vaccines company. Prior to September 11th we made vaccines for protecting travellers against cholera, typhoid fever and dysentery. We make antiviral vaccines for diarrhea in babies, for food safety, and we even have a vaccine that raises your HDL, your good cholesterol.

After September 11th, we moved to apply our advanced vaccine technologies to biodefense, as they have much to offer. For example, the current inventory anthrax vaccine provided to U.S. troops is administered through multiple injections, about 6 over about 18 months, which are often painful with side effects. And once the injections have begun, the protection develops gradually over several months. We think we can do better, and to my great pride we signed a contract in January that allows us to supply most advanced vaccine know-how to the biodefense effort. Under our contract with DVC, DynPort Vaccine Co., the prime contractor to the Defense Department's JVAP, Joint Vaccine Acquisition Program, we have begun development of a single-dose oral vaccine that will protect our troops against both anthrax and plague at the same time. This vaccine will have the same features as our cholera vaccine developed for the travellers' market, administered in a single oral dose, safe and well tolerated by the recipient, with immunity developing very rapidly in days, not weeks or months. Manufacture of this vaccine is easy and inexpensive to current—by comparison with current generation vaccines. And in addition, we can provide this in a form that does not require refrigeration.

Under the current plan we expect to complete preclinical development of this vaccine by the end of calendar year 2004. To my knowledge, it is the most advanced vaccine technology currently under development anywhere in the government's biodefense program, civilian or military.

So how does this experience shape my view of BioShield? Here are the central characteristics that I'll be looking for in BioShield. First, BioShield must create a market of sufficient size to convince the industry that we have a partner who understands the costs and complexity and risk of developing therapeutics and bringing them to market. Now, the research in any clinical stages may take tens of millions. But as you move through the final stages of clinical development over the finish line, it takes hundreds of millions, and biotech companies will want to see a Federal program of sufficient size to convince them that our effort can be funded throughout the life cycle of the program.

Second, there must be a long-term commitment of funding. The development of biomedical countermeasures takes time; 5 to 10 years is very aggressive, and more than 10 years is not uncommon, and although we are making quick progress on things such as anthrax and plague, there are other less well known agents that may become terrorist threats. And we have heard a lot of talk about SARS, and we have barely begun to work on that yet, though some of the technologies will apply. To meet the nuclear missile threat, the government has spent a minimum of $3 million annually for I think now 20 years. That kind of long-range commitment will convince companies that the government is serious about defeating biological threats.

Third, there must be careful coordination, and we touched on this earlier, among the agencies, including a program management function that can bridge the divide between the NIH and the early discovery and research phases and the procurement at the Department of Homeland Security. And one of the most experienced acquirers of complex products is the Department of Defense, and in the Department of Defense, in JVAP, they have a program management function that I think could well be applied through the life cycle of products as they progress through BioShield and bridge the gap between the NIH and the Department of Homeland Security.

Fourth, two of my colleagues have mentioned it, there must be adequate liability protection. I am not going to go into it further, but simply say that from the point of view of a small company, it isn't even a meritorious legal case that is a threat; even just the threat itself of liability is enough to prevent investment and put small companies out of business. So this is a risk that small companies simply can't take.

The bill introduced by Senators Lieberman and Hatch also provides for liability protection. Their legislation offers us protection in the context of comprehensive incentives for biotechs, and perhaps an approach like that can be incorporated into the BioShield concept of government-created markets that pull firms into this worthy effort.

So although I am very optimistic about the opportunity for success, I want to close with a personal experience that actually leaves my hope tinged with concern and, frankly, keeps me awake at night. We at AVANT have put huge amounts of resources into our program for a single-dose oral anthrax/plague vaccine, and we have a partner who is willing, the Joint Vaccine Acquisition Program, but we found that the 2004 budget has been slashed from the level it received in fiscal 2003. So even if we are successful and deliver absolutely on the contract that we have now for the preclinical 2-year program, I am very concerned about the future of what is a really outstanding vaccine approach, because, as you heard, there may be rather little incorporation of the Department of Defense programs into BioShield. So I want to be sure that this doesn't become an example of how, despite the best of intentions, failure of the many agencies involved to keep their coordinated eye on the biodefense ball could undermine effective programs and partnerships.

So I remain hopeful that working together the government and industry can make BioShield work for the national interest. I applaud your leadership in holding this hearing and meeting the challenge, and I assure you that our industry will be a willing partner.

Thank you very much, and I will be happy to answer questions.

Chairman TOM DAVIS. Thank you very much.

[The prepared statement of Ms. Ryan follows:]

AVANT
IMMUNOTHERAPEUTICS, INC.

Testimony of

Una S. Ryan, Ph.D.

President and CEO, AVANT Immunotherapeutics, Inc.

Before the House Government Reform Committee

Project BioShield Act of 2003

Friday, April 4, 2003

Mr. Chairman and Members of the Committee, thank you for inviting me to testify before you on Project BioShield. I am the President and CEO of AVANT Immunotherapeutics, Inc., a 60-person biotechnology firm headquartered in Needham, Massachusetts, with a division located in Overland, Missouri. I serve on the Board of Directors of the Biotechnology Industry Organization (BIO) and I am Vice-Chair of the Massachusetts Biotech Council, although I appear before you this morning exclusively in my capacity as AVANT's CEO. My comments are based, of course, on my experience as the CEO of a company that develops and produces vaccines that support the national biodefense effort, as a former research scientist at a large biotech company, Monsanto, and as an academic scientist for my entire professional career.

We sit this morning near ground zero of the war against bioterrorism. The last time I testified before members of this Committee, during a National Security Subcommittee hearing in October 2001, we had to convene at the Department of Health and Human Services, as House office buildings were closed due to possible anthrax contamination. Just across the Hill from where we sit is where the anthrax-laden letter addressed to Senator Daschle was opened; just over a mile away is the Brentwood facility where postal workers were lethally infected by the contents of that same letter. As awful as these events were, we all know that in some sense we were lucky in that a larger, coordinated, camouflaged anthrax attack could have been far deadlier. As the federal government embarks on BioShield, a new and innovative program to fight bioterrorism and biological warfare, let me assure you that the biotechnology industry stands ready to contribute and work towards its success.

Our eagerness to participate, however, cannot be unqualified. As the leader of a small company, I cannot embark on the development and supply of biodefense vaccines if doing so does not make business sense. I appear before you today to provide the perspective of a small biotechnology company on the concerns that my colleagues and I have about participating in the biodefense effort and how I hope Project BioShield will address them.

BioShield—A Small Biotech's View

Let me speak briefly of how the biodefense effort looks from my vantage point as the leader of a small biotech company. At AVANT, we develop a variety of therapies that harness the body's immune system, including a vaccine to manage cholesterol levels (raising HDL "good" cholesterol). The area of AVANT's work most relevant to the national biodefense effort is our development of vaccines that fight both bacterial and viral diseases. When it comes to vaccines, small companies like ours have much to offer. Vaccines have economics that scare away large pharmaceutical companies, who spend their research and development dollars seeking therapeutics that offer greater return. The vaccine world offers great opportunities for small companies like mine, for whom the promise of a smaller, yet distinct market offers reasonable return for the application of our cutting-edge scientific expertise.

Our vaccine business prior to September 11th focused on the market for travelers' vaccines—protecting against cholera, typhoid, and dysentery—and on anti-viral vaccines to combat diarrhea in babies. However, we have worked with the Department of Defense, in particular the Army, in the biodefense effort well before the fall of 2001. One result of that work was that in October 2001, AVANT licensed its recombinant protective antigen for anthrax to DynPort Vaccine Company (DVC) a Defense Department contractor developing a second-generation anthrax vaccine. This protective antigen is the crucial ingredient of an anthrax vaccine, the protein that prompts the body to develop immunity to the disease so that if the person is infected, it already has protective antibodies in its arsenal.

Although we are proud of this initial contribution to the biodefense effort, we are now playing a much more significant role. Our most advanced technology offers the prospect of biodefense vaccines that are far more effective, safer, less expensive, and faster acting than current generations of vaccines. For example, the current inventory anthrax vaccine provided to U.S. troops is administered through multiple injections, which are often painful because of the side effects of the vaccine. Once the series of injections is begun, immunity develops gradually over several months.

Compare this to the vaccine that we at AVANT, using our live attenuated vaccine vector technology, have successfully developed to fight cholera. This vaccine, called CholeraGarde, is administered in a single oral dose. It is safe and easily tolerated by the recipient. Immunity develops very quickly, in as little as 7 days. Manufacture of this vaccine is easy and inexpensive compared to current generation vaccines. While this particular vaccine fights cholera, our vector technology enables us to develop quickly a biodefense vaccine that is similarly effective, safe, and convenient. Our technology lets us adapt our vaccines to fight a wide range of bioterror agents.

To my great pride, we signed a contract in January that allows us to apply our most advanced vaccine know-how to the biodefense effort. Under our contract with DVC, the prime contractor to the Defense Department's Joint Vaccine Acquisition Program, we have begun development of a single-dose oral vaccine that will protect our troops against both anthrax and plague. As designed, the vaccine will have the same features of rapid protection and minimal side effects that characterize our commercial travelers' vaccines. Furthermore, using our proprietary VitriLife drying process, our vaccines will be storable in powdered form at room temperature, eliminating the cost and burden of refrigerated storage. Under the current plan, we expect to complete preclinical development of this vaccine by the end of calendar year 2004. To my knowledge, ours is the most advanced technology vaccine currently under development anywhere in the government's biodefense program, civilian or military.

Making BioShield Work—Size, Consistency, Transparency

How then, does this experience shape my view of BioShield? Let me discuss two major issues related to how BioShield will take shape that will affect its ability to attract biotechnology companies to participate.

My greatest concern revolves around whether the BioShield initiative and corresponding efforts at the Defense Department represent a long-term commitment on the part of the government of sufficient size to make the venture worthwhile for our companies. An assumption underpinning BioShield is that the federal government, not the private sector, must create a sufficient market to pull biotech companies into developing and producing biodefense countermeasures. For the government to create an adequate market, I believe it must ensure that BioShield will possess three key attributes pertaining to the size, scope, and durability of the program.

First, the market created by BioShield must be of sufficient size to convince the industry that we have a partner who understands the cost, complexity, and risk of developing therapeutics and bringing them to market. The development of a successful biomedical product costs in a range that begins in the tens of millions of dollars and extends into the hundreds of millions. Research and development activities are expensive, protracted clinical trials even more so. Initial indications are that the application of the animal testing rule by FDA, the process by which efficacy of biodefense vaccines will be tested, will entail significant Phase IV post-licensing clinical trials to ensure efficacy and safety. This all adds up to a sizable bill for each and every countermeasure that is developed, licensed, and employed. Biotech companies will want to see a federal program of sufficient size to convince them that our effort can be funded throughout the life cycle, and that the risk we endure and success we achieve will be fairly compensated.

The second necessary feature for a sufficient federal biodefense market is the long-term commitment of funding. As I mentioned, the development of biomedical countermeasures takes time. Five to ten years or more is not uncommon. Although we are making quick progress on anthrax, plague, and some other well-known agents, the broader list of agents includes many which are less well known and more technically challenging, such as viral agents and hemorrhagic fevers, like Ebola. I believe the government understands that meeting the biological weapons threat is of similar importance to the nuclear threat in many respects. The Strategic Defense Initiative, which celebrated its twentieth anniversary last month, launched a missile defense program whose funding has not dropped below $3 billion dollars annually over two decades. That kind of long-range commitment will convince companies that the government is a serious partner in this undertaking.

The third element of a reliable and consistent biodefense market is that it be run by a coordinated and transparent policy process, and that the policy itself be consistent over time. There will be two agencies playing the lead on BioShield, NIH for discovery and the Department of Homeland Security for procurement. For its part, the Defense Department will play both of these roles with respect to countermeasures for our troops. Careful coordination among the agencies will be crucial for developing clear and consistent policy. The industry understands that acquisition priorities must vary in response to evolving threats and advances in technology. To the extent attainable, however, acquisition priorities that remain consistent from year to year will boost our confidence that we have a reliable government partner. We look forward to working closely with the coordinating agencies to ensure that both the government and industry understand the goals, requirements, and preferences of its partners. In general, the greater the transparency and consistency in BioShield policy, the more readily it will attract biotech industry partners.

Department of Homeland Security Plays a Crucial Role

I would like to make one last comment regarding the market-creation challenge faced by BioShield. In some ways, the crucial role of the BioShield acquisition function will be played by the Department of Homeland Security. The NIH, with its responsibility for funding and promoting research into biodefense technologies, will be doing more of what it has long done so well. The biomedical procurement authority in this scheme will be the DHS, a role that none of its component bureaus has ever played. This is a daunting task for a well-established organization, not to mention a brand new department. We will be watching carefully to see that DHS is given the authority and funding it will need to fill this crucial role. If DHS is suitably empowered, the industry will sit up and take notice.

By enumerating these challenges, I am not trying to sound pessimistic. I believe that the goal of creating a market for biodefense of sufficient size and reliability to attract and maintain the participation of small biotech firms is eminently achievable. If this is achieved, the government will find us eager and committed partners. But we will be watching continuously to discern whether our partner is truly in it for the long haul. To meet these challenges, we are eager to work with the BioShield authorities as they shape the program over the months and years ahead to ensure that it meets the requirements of the federal government and industry, the surest route to a successful partnership.

Although I remain optimistic about the opportunity for success, I would like to mention a personal experience that indicates how the partnership can founder. At AVANT we have taken a considerable risk by devoting a sizable chunk of my young company's resources to our oral anthrax and plague vaccine project. We have found the Defense Department's Joint Vaccine Acquisition Program to be an excellent partner that has extensive understanding of the countermeasures development process, from start to finish. But already, our willing JVAP partner has found its FY 2004 budget slashed from the level it received in fiscal year 2003. Already I am up at night worrying whether even if we succeed in the first phase of our vaccine development, whether funding will be available to finish the preclinical segment, let alone enter into clinical trials. Seeing JVAP have its funding slashed makes no sense to me given the high priority placed on biodefense by both Congress and the Administration, as evidenced by this hearing today. I hope that this instance does not become an example of how, despite the best of intentions, failure of the many agencies involved to keep their coordinated eye on the biodefense ball could undermine effective programs and partnerships.

The Need for Liability Protections

After an adequate and reliable market, my second great concern revolves around indemnification. As in all business decisions, I can lead my company to accept risk only in return for a commensurate reward. I cannot envision a situation in which I could risk my stockholders' investments and my employees' livelihoods by venturing unprotected into the biodefense realm where large portions of the population will be inoculated in a program of administration over which we have little control. Our advanced technology vaccines have proved both safer and more effective than previous generation vaccines for the same diseases. Moreover, the FDA regulatory system sets the world standard for ensuring that only the safest and most effective therapeutics ever reach the American public. To then be vulnerable to lawsuits that could put us out of business just by their existence rather than their merit is a position in which I cannot place my company. There are many examples of product liability protection extended to companies that supply much-needed vaccines, most recently the protection offered by the Homeland Security Act to manufacturers of the smallpox vaccine. I believe I speak for most if not all of my colleagues in the industry when I say that unless we are protected from this risk to a fair and reasonable degree, we will not be able to participate in this national effort.

Mr. Chairman, My colleagues and I in the biotechnology industry have devoted our careers to creating products that serve the health and well being of the American public. I can think of no better way to continue that work than by playing a role in the BioShield program we discuss here today. BioShield is a comprehensive effort on the part of the Congress and the Administration to tackle the urgent and complex task of protecting the American people from biological threats. As a participant in this effort, I thank you and the entire Committee for your leadership. I hope that by laying out my concerns and requirements for a program in which my company and others like it will be able to participate that I have supported your efforts to devise an effective program. Thank you very much.

Chairman TOM DAVIS. Dr. Bowdish, thanks for being with us.

Ms. BOWDISH. Chairman Davis and distinguished members of the committee, I am honored to present this testimony on the application of monoclonal antibodies, the very latest biotech solution for defense against the very real threat of bioterrorism facing our Nation today. It's my understanding that the BioShield Initiative is designed to give key Federal agencies what amounts to fast-track authority for the review and approval of private sector solutions to fight the agents of bioterrorism. I wholeheartedly support the concept behind this and other legislative approaches such as the Lieberman-Hatch bill in the Senate. There is no better way to generate new therapies than to let the top people in their respective fields bring the best ideas to the table.

I know these legislative efforts importantly address long-term problems, but I also hope that NIH and other Federal agencies will take immediate steps that address the very real threats that we all face right now. As we saw in the attacks against our Nation in 2001, inhalation anthrax is a highly fatal disease if not identified early enough for antibiotics to be of use. Death usually occurs within a few days of the onset of acute symptoms, primarily from the toxins produced by the anthrax bacteria, not the bacteria itself.

In addition to antibiotics directed against the bacteria, successful anthrax defense will require agents against the toxins otherwise known as antitoxins. Monoclonal antibodies are among the most logical and natural antitoxins that could be developed for the treatment of anthrax. Human monoclonal antibodies have been proven safe and effective for many therapeutic purposes, and I am confident that they will have similar success as bioterror antitoxins.

Alexion has successfully isolated human monoclonal antibodies with therapeutic potential for biodefense. For over a year we have had antibodies that could provide the most complete protection from anthrax toxin available. These antibodies, either alone or in combination, may be useful as a prophylactic at the onset or during or at the course of an active infection. As detailed in the written testimony, this work has been discussed with and presented to a large number of scientific experts on anthrax and biodefense in industry, academia and government. All of these individuals agree that the approach we are taking is a necessary and achievable component to U.S. biodefense initiatives.

Alexion's biodefense program against anthrax has been entirely self-supported to date. We saw a need, and we recognize that we had the ability to offer our technology and our expertise. And most importantly, we have demonstrated that our approach works. It is our hope that Congress can help us ensure that the appropriate decisionmakers in our Federal Government are aware of our critical and highly relevant work for consideration for civilian and military defense.

It is our desire to coordinate with government officials to see that our antibodies and our expertise are utilized for emergency stockpile generation to protect both the civilian and military populations. Building the necessary emergency stockpiles is certainly something that no one company can or should accomplish solely with private funding. Therefore, we are looking for assistance from the Federal Government through NIH for the final phase of development of this critical therapy.

Further, we are currently applying the same technology to additional agents of bioterror in our research laboratories. Preliminary results suggest we will have similar successes with smallpox, botulinum, plague and others. At the minimum, we hope emergency stockpiles of monoclonal antitoxins would deter would-be terrorists and alleviate public anxiety. Above all it is my hope we never have to look back from another bioterror attack and wonder what more could we have done and why did we wait.

I thank the committee for this opportunity to present this testimony, and I welcome any questions.

Chairman TOM DAVIS. Thank you very much.

Dr. Edwards.

Dr. EDWARDS. Chairman Davis and members of the committee, thank you for inviting the Infectious Diseases Society of America [IDSA], to present our views on the administration's Project BioShield. I am Dr. John Edwards, a professor of medicine at the School of Medicine at UCLA, and chief of the division of infectious disease at the Los Angeles County/Harbor-UCLA Medical Center.

Before I begin, I want to thank Dr. Fauci for his work on Project BioShield and his work at infectious diseases in general. He is a member of our society.

I am testifying today on behalf of the IDSA to convey our strong support for Project BioShield and the novel incentives it creates. However, the United States' most pressing infectious disease problems are not limited to infections that terrorists may propagate. An immediate crisis exists currently in U.S. hospitals and in our communities as naturally occurring infections become increasingly resistant to approved antimicrobial products. Additionally, naturally occurring infectious diseases exemplified by meningitis pneumonia, tuberculosis and AIDS are still the leading cause of death worldwide and the third leading cause of death in the United States. Furthermore, emerging infections such as Severe Acute Respiratory Syndrome [SARS], and West Nile virus are continuing threats.

Antimicrobial resistance whereby microbes mutate and become less susceptible to drugs has created special concerns. You probably know of the cases of vancomycin-resistant Staphylococcus aureus [VRSA], that occurred in Michigan and Pennsylvania last year. This occurrence is highly significant since vancomycin is typically a last resort agent. Similarly methicillin-resistant Staphy aureus, which previously affected mainly hospitalized patients, now is infecting healthy and strong individuals and communities across our country. Upon this background, the IDSA has learned that a, "perfect storm," if you will, is brewing as many pharmaceutical companies are considering or already have withdrawn from anti-infective drug development. Many companies have greatly curtailed, wholly eliminated or spun off their anti-infective research components especially over the last 5 years. A list of these major pharmaceutical companies is provided in our written statement.

Antimicrobials work often quickly and with successful results. Understandably, pharmaceutical and biotechnology companies are inclined to develop products that treat long-term chronic illnesses because such products provide greater returns on investment. As

U.S. demographics shift toward a more elderly population, we predict that companies will focus even more on chronic diseases in the future. Within the context of these realities, it is highly unlikely we can reverse the antimicrobial market failure without some form of specific well-designed intervention. Therefore, a national solution is needed to solve this national crisis.

Project BioShield's long-term legacy will be enhanced significantly if it is amended to address the precipitous decline in the development of antimicrobial products to treat naturally occurring and resistant infections.

Such amendments are supported by recommendations made by the Institute of Medicine in the Microbial threats report issued on March 18th. Thousands more Americans will succumb to naturally occurring infections in the next 10 to 15 years than to agents of bioterrorism, even if a bioterrorism attack occurs, and yet no plan is currently on the table to address this immediate public health crisis.

We strongly support the concept Project BioShield, but we unequivocally urge that it be amended to include a framework for action to protect Americans against naturally occurring and drug-resistant and emerging infections that are increasingly present in our hospitals and communities.

Chairman Davis, in your opening statement, you asked how can BioShield assist to address the SARS outbreak. In its current form, its assistance would be tangential. However, with amendments it could do much.

In closing, we sincerely thank the chairman and all members of the committee for the opportunity to discuss the urgent need for new technologies and tools to protect U.S. citizens and global populations from both the threat of bioterrorism and the highly prevalent naturally occurring infections.

The IDSA is available to assist in any way that it can. Thank you for sharing these concerns with us.

Chairman TOM DAVIS. Thank you very much, Dr. Edwards.

[The prepared statement of Dr. Edwards follows:]

IDSA
Infectious Diseases Society of America

Statement of the
Infectious Diseases Society of America (IDSA)
concerning "Project Bioshield"

Presented by
John E. Edwards, MD

Before the Government Reform Committee
U.S. House of Representatives

April 4, 2003

Chairman Davis, Representative Waxman and Members of the Committee, thank you for inviting the Infectious Diseases Society of America (IDSA) to present our views on the Administration's "Project Bioshield" initiative. I am Dr. John Edwards, a professor of medicine at the UCLA School of Medicine and chief of the Division of Infectious Diseases at the Los Angeles County/Harbor – UCLA Medical Center. I also serve as chair of IDSA's Public Policy Committee. I am testifying today on behalf of IDSA to communicate our strong support for Project Bioshield and the novel incentives it creates that will motivate research into and development of pharmaceuticals, vaccines and diagnostics that may be used to minimize and limit the devastation that a bioterrorism event may sow.

IDSA represents more than 7,000 domestic and international physicians and scientists devoted to patient care, education, research, and community health planning in infectious diseases (ID). Many of our members are researchers who study infectious microbes, including agents of bioterrorism as well as naturally occurring microbes. Many of our members also are involved in the development of new pharmaceuticals and vaccines to control, prevent and treat such infections. ID physicians will be integrally involved should a bioterrorism event occur; an ID specialist discovered the first anthrax case that occurred in Florida. In addition, over the past year, IDSA and its members—including those who were on the frontline of smallpox eradication efforts—have been key consultants to the federal and state governments as they have prepared responses to a potential smallpox event. Presently, many of our members are working closely with state and local public health officials to oversee the National Smallpox Immunization Program's implementation.

As abhorent as the thought may be to those of us here today, it is highly probable that terrorists are working in several corners of the world to produce infectious agents that may be untreatable, because of existing therapeutic and technological limitations. This is a threat of the most serious magnitude. IDSA believes strongly that more must be done to prepare the United States and the world for bioterrorism. Project Bioshield takes us in the right direction by providing important incentives, including funds, which we hope will accelerate pharmaceutical research into and development of new diagnostics, vaccines and therapeutics.

66 Canal Center Plaza • Suite 600 • Alexandria, VA 22314
TEL: (703) 299-0200 • FAX: (703) 299-0204
info@idsociety.org • www.idsociety.org

I am here today on behalf of ID physicians and experts to state clearly and unequivocally, however, that our concerns are not limited to infections that terrorists may propagate. A related and more immediate crisis is unfolding in U.S. hospitals and in our communities in the form of naturally occurring infections that are becoming increasingly resistant to existing antimicrobial drug products. Presently, naturally occurring infectious diseases are the second leading cause of death and the leading cause of disability-adjusted life years worldwide (one disability-adjusted life year equals one lost year of healthy life) and the third leading cause of death in the United States (A. Fauci, 2001). These serious and often life-threatening infections include meningitis, pneumonia, diarrheal illnesses, skin and bone infections, tuberculosis, malaria, hepatitis, sexually transmitted infections (i.e., gonorrhea and syphyllis) and HIV/AIDS. Additionally, they include new and emerging infections, such as the Severe Acute Respiratory Syndrome (SARS) and West Nile virus.

Antimicrobial resistance is the phenomenon whereby infectious microbes mutate and become less susceptible to treatment with currently approved drugs. Of greatest importance to ID physicians is preserving the effectiveness of drugs that are reserved for use as the last line of defense against certain infections. You probably have read about the cases of vancomycin resistant *Staphylococcus* aureus (VRSA) that occurred in Michigan in July 2002 and Pennsylvania in October 2002. The emergence of VRSA is of great concern to clinicians and public health officials as vancomycin is typically the drug of last resort in treating *S. aureus* and several other infections. The Centers for Disease Control and Prevention describes the Michigan case in an article published yesterday, April 3, 2003, in the New England Journal of Medicine. You also probably have heard about community associated methicillin resistant *Staphylococcus aureus (MRSA)*. MRSA, in the recent past, only affected immune-compromised individuals and the elderly in hospital settings. Now, it is occurring across the country in local communities – infecting healthy and strong individuals.

The problems posed by naturally occurring infections and amplified by antimicrobial resistance is frightening—but our immediate worries don't end there. IDSA has learned that a perfect storm is brewing as many drug companies are considering or already have withdrawn from antiinfective drug development. Aventis, Bristol-Myers Squibb, Lilly, GlaxoSmithKline, Procter & Gamble, Roche, and Wyeth have greatly curtailed, wholly eliminated or spun off their antiinfective research components over the past four years. Without new research into and development of new antimicrobial pharmaceuticals, the arsenal of weapons available to fight emerging and resistant microbes will diminish rapidly.

Although IDSA is concerned that tools are lacking to treat, prevent and diagnose many varieties of infection, the decline of pharmaceutical research into and development of *antibacterial drugs* is of particular concern to us. Bacterial diseases are a major contributor to infectious diseases-related illnesses and deaths worldwide. Industry withdrawals from this market will have devastating results for patients suffering from bacterial infections as well as for U.S. public health and global health, in general. Of significant note, in 2002, out of 89 new medicines emerging on the market, no new antibacterial drugs were approved. Since 1998, only seven new antibacterials have been approved. Current annual reports for the major pharmaceutical companies (Merck, Pfizer, GlaxoSmithKline, Bristol-Myers Squibb, Aventis, Abbot, AstraZeneca, Lilly, Roche, Johnson & Johnson, and Novartis) list only five new antibacterials in the drug pipeline out of more than 400 agents in development. Realizing that many years (frequently seven to ten) and significant investments are required to develop these agents, there will be an exceedingly small number, if any, new antibacterial products approved during the next five to ten years.

These data illustrate an ominously bleak picture. Antimicrobial drugs provide substantial and significant benefits to U.S. public health. These products are used everyday in emergency situations across the country and around the world. They often have been referred to as "miracle drugs" because of their ability to work quickly to save patients with serious or lethal infections. This "miracle" status is a double-edged sword. Because these products work quickly with successful results, they are rarely needed for long-term use. Understandably, pharmaceutical and biotechnology companies are much more inclined to develop products that treat long-term, chronic illnesses because such products provide greater returns on investment. Reversing the antimicrobial development failure, without some form of specific, well-designed intervention, appears unlikely, particularly as U.S. demographics shift toward an increasingly older population and products needed to treat chronic diseases suffered by the aged present more alluring opportunities for investors.

The growing body of evidence indicates that without immediate action, we simply will have fewer and fewer antimicrobial products available to treat an increasing number of infectious microbes at a time when resistance to available agents is exploding and new life-threatening infections are emerging.

<u>A National Solution to a National Problem</u>

IDSA believes Project Bioshield's impact may be strengthened significantly by amending it to address this precipitous decline in antimicrobial drug development. Policymakers in the Administration developed Project Bioshield as a new approach to address a serious national security crisis--bioterrorism. Bioshield offers a logical solution to the market failure that exists in the area of biodefense. Project Bioshield also demonstrates federal policymakers' capacity to develop quickly a framework for action and solutions when crises threaten the United States. Bioshield's incentives will motivate industry to develop new products that will protect us from bioterrorism agents as well as decrease national security risks created by threats of bioterrorism.

The decline of private investments into antimicrobial research and development and the increasing development of highly resistant infectious strains, coupled with the emergence of new infectious diseases, create a crisis situation that cries out for a similar immediate and long-term solution. Thousands more Americans will succumb to naturally occurring infections in the next ten to fifteen years than to agents of bioterrorism. Yet, no plan is on the table to address this immediate public health crisis.

Amending the "Project Bioshield Act of 2003" to include incentives to motivate the production of new tools to address this public health crisis can positively change market dynamics that presently are on a downward spiral. As currently drafted, the "Project Bioshield Act of 2003" does support the creation of a novel framework to address immediate public health crises. In Section 4 of the Act, the Food and Drug Administration is authorized to permit use of an unapproved drug in an actual or potential emergency, if the Secretary of Health and Human Services determines that a "specified disease or condition" *unrelated to terrorism* creates an emergency situation. However, the Act does not pay similar deference to public health emergencies in Section 2, which provides the National Institutes of Health the power to speed research and development activities, or Section 3, which establishes novel incentives to motivate the pharmaceutical industry to develop new products.

It is important to note that biodefense efforts also can benefit from strengthening Bioshield to support the development of new public health tools. Experts believe it is highly likely that individuals are working to develop drug resistant strains of common infections (e.g., tuberculosis, etc.). Thus, expansion of Bioshield's scope to include incentives for development of new drugs to treat these common infections, and particularly, drug resistant strains of common infections, will have favorable implications in the bioterrorism context.

In closing, we sincerely thank the Chairman and all Members of the Committee for the opportunity to discuss the urgency for new technologies and tools to protect the U.S. and global populations from the threat of both bioterrorism and naturally occurring infections. We strongly support the concept of Project Bioshield, but we unequivocally urge that it be amended to include a framework for action to protect Americans against infections that are occurring daily in our hospitals and communities. The federal government, pharmaceutical and biotechnology industries, the medical community, and ordinary people all have a stake in the outcome—but without quick action public health and patient care are at risk. IDSA and its expert members are available to assist in you in any way that we can.

Chairman TOM DAVIS. The point you make, that with some amendments we may be able to shape this legislation up where it can help us with the SARS or the next Ebola or whatever, is very, very important.

Sometimes we get an opportunity like this legislatively when we want to make it as inclusive as we can. So I think your point is well taken.

We don't know what will happen from a bioterrorism point of view over the next decade. Hopefully nothing. But there are going to continue to be SARS and mutations and things that the private marketplace is going to be reluctant to get into without strong Federal help.

And having a system up that could include these areas, I think would be very, very helpful. So we will take all of your comments into account as we try to write this legislation and move it through.

I am concerned, and I am—I guess I will ask everybody. Putting—if we get this fund up, we put limited liability and the other things that are asked for in the legislation, a concern of an unintended consequence downstream being that all of a sudden putting so much into biomedical countermeasures, could it affect other biomedical research into more conventional areas?

Can you find pharmacy companies all of a sudden putting their research into these areas where you have a guaranteed fund at the end that will pay for these, instead of taking the chance in the marketplace, and how will this affect more conventional research and development?

Dr. FRIEDMAN. Thank you. I will begin. I am sure others will join in as well.

The problem is, in a sense, caused by the fact that there are so many opportunities that are available. These are opportunities that have been made available because of the scientific investments that have been made in this country over the last 40 or 50 years.

I think it is true to say that whether you are talking about an academic medical center, a pharmaceutical company, a large pharmaceutical company or a small company, there are vastly more promising ideas for helping people today than we have the time, the energy, the resources, the expertise or the dollars.

And that is a continuing challenge for us all. As was pointed out, one of the reasons why pharmaceutical manufacturers have been putting less emphasis on infectious disease over the last decade is that there have been more urgent public health opportunities, cancer, Alzheimer's, other very serious diseases, where companies thought that important investments made there would help more patients.

As we have come to recognize that the threats to our health change, we must rebalance the equation. There are no simple answers. There aren't enough resources or people or time to address all of the scientific and medical questions that legitimately exist. It is a real challenge for all of us to try and define what that right balance is.

We must make those assessments and then we must constantly reevaluate and question those and decide how we can make the greatest contribution to the public health, with which source of investments of our energy and time and people.

Chairman TOM DAVIS. I mean, in all fairness, you want to make contributions to public health, but you have a bottom line to your shareholders too. And if the money is available out there in these—in some of these other areas, it may be a more sure investment than some of the other areas.

Dr. FRIEDMAN. It is theoretically possible. I think by far the more driving consideration will be how likely it is to be successful. So if we have a wonderful insight into multiple sclerosis or diabetes, the opportunity to contribute there—as you are well aware, because you understand this, there is a huge number of things that are screened and begin testing, and a tiny, tiny percentage that end up—not because people are sloppy or because they don't care, because we don't have the biological insights. As sophisticated as we are, we are not sophisticated enough.

Chairman TOM DAVIS. This is tough stuff. Dr. Ryan.

Dr. RYAN. I think the unintended consequences will be all benefits. If you look at the countermeasures and the technologies we can offer now, they were all built on peacetime research and activities.

And much of what I think we would benefit from in developing needle-free, nonrequiring-refrigeration vaccines, would be equally useful for travelers' vaccines, food safety vaccines, vaccines for global health. So it is the same intellectual property and technology that we would be leveraging into another area. So I would see all of the boats rising, and I wouldn't see competition being a problem at all.

Chairman TOM DAVIS. All right. Thanks.

For a countermeasure to be appropriate for procurement under the Project BioShield as envisioned by the administration, the Secretary of Health and Human Services has to make a determination that the product is either approved by the FDA or is likely to be approved within 5 years.

Is that a reasonable approach? And what type of products would be covered by this timeframe? And what type do you think would be excluded by this timeframe? Any thoughts on that?

Ms. BOWDISH. I believe that monocromial antibodies will be able to be approved in this timeframe. I think that in our case, speaking from a small-company perspective, we already have antitoxin therapy available for anthrax. I think it will take us the next 6 months to get it through the next series of studies that we need to do, and then likely into phase 1 safety studies.

I think that our approach will be successful against the other agents that we are working on now and will be working on in the future. I think that we can very quickly have a rapid success with antitoxin therapies and antiviral therapies in the case of monocromial antibodies.

Chairman TOM DAVIS. Thank you. One of the areas you are going to see debated on both sides of this is, are we giving away too much to the companies? Are we in fact not being tough enough, that they are going to walk off with big profits? Are we giving them too many protections and the like?

But the bottom line for us is to be able to get incentives so the companies will step forward, take the risk, do the research. It is clear from the last panel that government doesn't have this in-house capability. We have got to go out to private sector.

We can write a law here that may have all kinds of safeguards and protections so that the government isn't getting taken. But if companies don't step up to the plate, the losers at the end of the day are going to be the consumers and people are who are suffering from this.

What we wrestle here with is striking the right balance. As we look at the administration's proposal, does it have enough incentives for private companies to begin research and development? Do you think it has enough? Do you think it needs more? Do you think it goes too far? We ought to bring other safeguards in? I think all of you have different perspectives on that. But does anybody want to take that?

Dr. FRIEDMAN. Very briefly, sir. I think there are some incentives that are being discussed. I think equally important is addressing the disincentives that exist to try and optimize the system. I think that at the totality of what we are trying to create for the American public balances careful discussions.

These are complicated issues. And, as others have said, we look forward to working with you and others to try and craft this. Specifically, where there are special descriptions in the legislation, we think those should be transparent, they should be clear, and they should be well focused.

Chairman TOM DAVIS. OK. Thank you. Anyone else on that?

Dr. RYAN. What I like about the 5-year idea is that there is a clear philosophy to support product opportunities, not just support research.

What I don't like about the 5 years is I think it is a bit tight. I mean, if somebody is progressing extremely well, I think it would not be useful to the country to cut it off if it went another couple of years.

Chairman TOM DAVIS. So, some waiver extension?

Dr. RYAN. A question of progress. Again, as I keep stressing, program management through the life cycle from research to having a product that could actually be used.

Chairman TOM DAVIS. I mean, your company spends a lot of money that sometimes ends up going nowhere, right, with the research?

Dr. RYAN. Oh, yeah.

Chairman TOM DAVIS. What percent? As you go off on a trail, how much times does it lead nowhere?

Dr. RYAN. Most of the time, is the depressing thought. But in fact the research is still useful. Others studies have been done, not just by my company, but when you get to the end of the road, it is 1 in 100 is what makes it through to success.

Dr. FRIEDMAN. I think it depends where you start. It could be as small as 1 in 10,000 or 100,000 if you look at the very earliest steps, when something begins clinical testing. You are happy if it is 1 in 100. Again, this is not just for anti-infectives, but for a variety of different medications.

Mr. RAPOPORT. Mr. Chairman, I think the incentives are there, but they need to be firmed up. And let me give you a specific example. In the last anthrax procurement, which was won by a company whose name I can't recall, but the basic provision, the RFP, was for research and development only.

So you stand back, and you are chairman of a multinational drug company. And you look at, am I going to do research and development? I would love to help. I want to be there. In fact, it looks like the government is paying my way.

What happens at the end of the contract? Nothing. You get no widget. You get no promise. In fact, the procurement said there will be another RFP at the end of the research and development. And you wonder, as outside counsel, how do you advise your company on, well, do you get the rights to the work that has been developed by the other companies that have won the R&D?

So it is very simple in the sense that if you want to attract companies like Aventis, I think they are willing to share the risk, but they need to know that if they show you their stuff and they are successful, there is a guarantee that there is going to be a market there.

It is as if to say we fight a war in Iraq, and Boeing is not there, Lockheed is not there, Northrup is not there. We have got some very sophisticated companies, but we need some of the big players with unlimited resources to participate in this as well.

Chairman TOM DAVIS. Thank you. I mean, that is the American system. There is a huge up-side when you get success. If you don't get success, you end up eating the cost. But there is a huge up-side. And what you are saying here is there is no assurance of that in some of these cases. Thank you very much.

Mr. Waxman.

Mr. WAXMAN. Thank you, Mr. Chairman.

I want to thank all of the witnesses for their testimony. I had a conflict in my time schedule so I wasn't here to hear you, but I have had a chance to review the testimony and will certainly take into consideration all of the things that you have given us because I think it is very helpful.

Mr. Rapoport, you testified you assumed checks and balances are in place to ensure appropriate stewardship to protect the taxpayers' money. It seems to me that the bill eliminates many guarantees to protect the taxpayers' interest: eliminating government access; rights to the books of contractors, for instance, seems questionable.

What kind of checks do you think are in place?

Mr. RAPOPORT. I noticed from your earlier question that you were concerned about that. Remember, the simplified acquisition is only up to $25 million. After that, the full panoply of Federal Acquisition Regulations, with the masses of government auditors that are already over the pharmaceutical industry, they will be there.

In my days at the Justice Department, we had the FBI, we had the IG. There is everybody there from those enforcers to the contracting officials who ask for one thing: Get the stuff out the back door. As long as you can keep producing, there will be no audits.

So the $25 million, quite frankly, is a very low number to receive a relaxation of government acquisition enforcement. Most of this will be far in excess of $25 million.

Mr. WAXMAN. Well, the production side, however, it is not limited to that $25 million.

Mr. RAPOPORT. It is our view that the production side doesn't even have this simplified acquisition in it. There is no relaxation. There is total—in fact, it is a very aggressive position which says that if you don't produce, Mr. Pharmaceutical Co., within 3 years, we are going to terminate you for default. That didn't have to be in there. There is already that ample authority under the FAR.

Mr. WAXMAN. You have testified that companies need the certainty that research and development contracts will lead to a manufacturing agreement. This is an important part as far you can see to tie the two together?

Mr. RAPOPORT. Yes. We are not assuming that the price has to be decided until later in the contract. But the government does this type of price determination midway through a procurement all of the time.

Mr. WAXMAN. Do companies make money on research and development contracts? And, if so, why would you need a guarantee of a manufacturing agreement up front?

Mr. RAPOPORT. There is probably a difference between a company like Aventis and a biotech. We are not anxious to accept government money, as you suggest. We are not government contractors. The pharmacy industry, I guess the Wall Street Journal calls them the new biodefense contractors.

But a large pharmaceutical company wouldn't have the institutional competency to deal with what Boeing and Lockheed has. So they are not anxious to take government R&D money simply to earn a 7 or 8 percent profit on top of the R&D. It is the manufacturing capability that they want, and that they are best at, that they deliver. That is really why they are where they are.

So at the beginning when I said our tinkering with the bill—and it is a good bill—is simply not only to encourage biotechs who absolutely have to be there, but also the companies that have the ability to produce masses of quantities of vaccines. And they don't need the government's R&D money as long as they know that there is some kind of back-end commitment.

Mr. WAXMAN. Dr. Friedman, good to see you again. You have indicated the importance of the liability protection. Why wouldn't the government contractor defense shield you from liability?

Dr. FRIEDMAN. I am sorry, sir?

Mr. WAXMAN. You indicated that—the concern about the potential liability companies manufacturing these countermeasure could face, and their inability to retain private insurance. I am trying to understand why wouldn't the government contractor defense shield be adequate for protection?

Dr. FRIEDMAN. This is an area that skirts my expertise in terms of legal understanding. But as it has been explained to me, and I believe it is accurate, the indemnification activities that exist for many kinds of contractural procedures are really not anywhere near as flexible or appropriate or useful as some of the liability kinds of protections that exist.

I believe the recent example of how smallpox has been dealt with is a very reasonable model for us to take forward. And if I may just expand on my answer for a moment, to answer a question not—that you didn't address to me, but you did address earlier, because I really feel it is worth some further discussion.

Our feeling is that the liability protection should be afforded not just to the manufacturer. We think there is a very strong case for that. I am happy to further define that. But we also believe that there should be some equitable, appropriate consideration of the people who are receiving the product, and, I would even add, the people who are delivering the product; that is, the health care providers, physicians and so forth.

The reason is I think that we are operating—anytime you have a product considered, even approved by the Food and Drug Administration, there is a balance of what we know and what we don't know.

At a certain point the FDA and its scientists say, we know enough to say that this is relatively safe and relatively effective, because there is nothing that is absolutely safe and absolutely effective. And we have confidence when there is a lot of information there.

Our concern is that for some of these products, because of the difficulty of testing them, because of the fact that they may be in the midst of development, that balance will be shifted and we won't know quite as much as we would like to. And there will be more unknowns about risks and benefits.

Mr. WAXMAN. So you think that the manufacturers should be protected from liability to give the incentive to development of these products, but the public that is exposed to them, that may have some adverse effects, should also be compensated?

Dr. FRIEDMAN. Yes, sir.

Mr. WAXMAN. Dr. Edwards, I want to welcome you because you are from UCLA, among other reasons. There was a report in yesterday's New England Journal of Medicine that a common bacteria is now highly resistant to Vancomycin, one of the most powerful antibiotics in modern medicine.

Do you believe that more research needs to be done to find alternative treatment for Vancomycin-resistant bacteria?

Dr. EDWARDS. Absolutely. This is just a major problem that we are facing every day in our hospitals. And in fact, I would like to give a very brief example that sort of summarizes a conundrum. In our institution we recently had a patient who was a 60-year-old, brought in by her family, her daughter and her grandchildren, and had severe asthma and also had evidence of an infection that seemed to be mild. A deliberate decision was made not to put the patient on Vancomycin, because that drug has become so valuable, and there is so little in the background available to counteract the Vancomycin-resistant organism.

So the patient was relatively stable at the time she came into the hospital. But she rapidly decompensated and died, unfortunately. And at the time of her autopsy, an organism that was multiplying resistantly to antimicrobials was recovered, but it was sensitive to Vancomycin.

And this example illustrates how we are faced with the situation now of trying to conserve the use of specifically that agent, but also others, because there is so very little in the background for support for resistant organisms.

And the situation is very complex and intricate. And I think this example displays some of those intricacies of the kinds of decisions that are being made in hospitals all over the country now based on this resistance problem.

Mr. WAXMAN. Do you think there are natural security implications?

Dr. EDWARDS. Absolutely. The resistance issue is tied to some of the basic science of bioterrorism agents as well.

Mr. WAXMAN. Thank you. That is very helpful to have on the record.

Thank you very much, Mr. Chairman. And I want to thank the panel.

Chairman TOM DAVIS. I want to thank the panel as well. It has been very helpful to us as we try to formulate some meaningful legislation over the next few months.

Anyone want to add anything before we go? If not, let me just again thank you. I want to thank the staff for working on this hearing. We will be following up on a SARS issue at a hearing scheduled for next Wednesday, April 9th, at 10 a.m.

We will keep the record open for 2 weeks if you want to supplement your comments. If you think of anything you didn't say or respond to, please feel free to do that. And the hearing is adjourned. Thank you.

[Whereupon, at 11:50 a.m., the committee was adjourned.]

[Additional information submitted for the hearing record follows:]

Record

HGS
Human Genome Sciences, Inc.
9410 Key West Avenue
Rockville, MD 20850

Testimony of
Human Genome Sciences, Inc.
Submitted to the United States House of Representatives
Committee on Government Reform

April 4, 2003

Hearing on the Project BioShield Act of 2003

Mr. Chairman, members of the Committee, thank you for your invitation to submit this testimony on behalf of Human Genome Sciences, Inc., which has discovered a promising new drug to prevent and treat anthrax infections. Specifically, Human Genome Sciences has developed a human monoclonal antibody – called ABthrax™ – that is effective in protecting against anthrax in multiple experimental animal models.

ABthrax

Human Genome Sciences, Inc., founded in 1992, is a pioneer in the use of genomics, the systematic collection and understanding of human genes and their functions, for the discovery and development of new pharmaceutical products. Our mission is to treat and cure disease by bringing new gene-based drugs to patients, and we currently have eight drugs in human clinical trials. Our primary focus has *not* been the development of drugs to protect against attack by biological and chemical weapons. Nevertheless, just over sixteen months ago, we realized that Human Genome Sciences had the technology and capability to develop a human monoclonal antibody drug to block the lethal effects of the anthrax toxin. As a company headquartered just outside Washington D.C., we witnessed first-hand the potentially devastating effects of the use of anthrax as a terrorist weapon in late 2001.

Anthrax infection is caused by a spore-forming bacterium, *Bacillus anthracis,* which multiplies in the body and produces lethal toxins. Most anthrax fatalities are caused by the irreversible effects of the anthrax toxins. Indeed, the Committee on Government Reform held a hearing last year on "Quickening the Pace of Research in Protecting Against Anthrax and Other Biological Terrorist Agents" that focused primarily on "toxin interference."[1] At that hearing, then-Chairman Dan Burton stated that, "Finding better treatments [for anthrax] like anti-toxins is vital,"[2] and Congressman Christopher Shays, among other members of the Committee, noted that, "A sharper focus on development of anti-toxins is warranted, some might say overdue, because anthrax has long been acknowledged as the most likely biological weapon threat."[3]

Human Genome Sciences has developed such an anti-toxin. Research has shown that protective antigen is the key facilitator in the progression of anthrax infection at the cellular level.[4] After protective antigen and the other anthrax toxins are produced by the bacteria, protective antigen binds to the anthrax toxin receptor on cell surfaces and forms a protein-receptor complex that makes it possible for the anthrax toxins to enter the cells. ABthrax blocks the binding of protective antigen to cell surfaces and prevents the anthrax toxins from entering and killing the cells.

Currently, two options are available for the prevention or treatment of anthrax infections – a vaccine and antibiotics. Both are essential to dealing with anthrax, but both have limitations. The anthrax vaccine takes several weeks following the first doses before immunity is initially established. The vaccine also requires multiple injections over a period of eighteen months, in addition to annual boosters, to maintain its protective effect. Antibiotics are effective in killing

---

1 See *Quickening the Pace of Research in Protecting Against Anthrax and Other Biological Terrorist Agents: A Look at Toxin Interference Before the House Comm. on Government Reform*, 107th Cong., H.R. MISC DOC. NO. 107-64 (Feb. 28, 2002).

2 *Id.* at 2.

3 *Id.* at 15.

4 Inglesby TV, O'Toole T, Henderson DA, et al. Anthrax as a Biological Weapon, 2002: Updated recommendations for Management. JAMA May, 2002. 287(17): 2236-2252.

anthrax bacteria, but are not effective against the anthrax toxins once those toxins have been released into the blood. Antibiotics also may not be effective against antibiotic-resistant strains of anthrax.

In ABthrax, Human Genome Sciences has discovered a third defense against anthrax infections. In contrast to the anthrax vaccine, a single dose of ABthrax confers protection immediately following the rapid achievement of appropriate blood levels of the antibody. In contrast to antibiotics, ABthrax is effective against the lethal toxins released by anthrax bacteria. It may also prevent and treat infections by antibiotic-resistant strains of anthrax.

Results from preclinical studies conducted to date demonstrate that a single dose of ABthrax administered prophylactically increases survival significantly in both rabbits and nonhuman primates exposed by inhaling lethal doses of anthrax spores. In both models, we observed an absence of bacteria in the blood of all ABthrax-treated animals that survived. The rabbit and nonhuman primate models of inhalation anthrax are regarded as sufficient to demonstrate the efficacy of therapeutic and prophylactic agents in treating or preventing anthrax infection. A single dose of ABthrax also fully protected rats against a lethal challenge with the anthrax toxins. Full results of these studies will be disclosed in upcoming scientific meetings and publications as appropriate.

Based on our preclinical results to date, we believe that ABthrax has the potential to be used both prophylactically and therapeutically. For example, ABthrax may be used to protect rescuers entering a contaminated building, soldiers in an infected environment, or exposed individuals after an attack. In addition, post-exposure treatment may lessen the natural progression of anthrax infection and increase survival. Human Genome Sciences plans to file an Investigational New Drug application in the near future, seeking clearance from the U.S. Food and Drug Administration (FDA) to begin clinical trials to evaluate the safety, tolerability, and pharmacology of ABthrax in healthy adults.

Project BioShield

The utility of Project BioShield and the ability of private companies to develop viable defenses against bioterrorism threats are demonstrated by Human Genome Sciences' expeditious development of ABthax. According to the White House overview of Project Bioshield:

> "Scientific breakthroughs such as recombinant DNA technology, immunology, molecular structural engineering, genomics, and proteomics that are now protecting our health from many conventional diseases hold considerable promise against the diseases of terrorism as well. This same innovation can be applied to the challenge of protecting America by identifying the new treatments that are most needed, and providing meaningful and consistent rewards for innovators who bring these products to the American public."[5]

Many companies, such as Human Genome Sciences, have the capability and are willing to develop new products to protect against attack by biological and chemical weapons or other dangerous pathogens, but they need the assurance that a market exists for such drugs. In most cases, the only potential market is the federal government and, potentially, our foreign allies.

With respect to ABthrax, Human Genome Sciences is at a critical stage. The company is ready to transition the drug to production, which will require significant investment to secure a manufacturing facility and perfect the manufacturing process. Due to the demand for such specialized facilities, a delay of months now could postpone delivery of the drug by over a year. We are also ready to begin clinical safety trials in humans, having already demonstrated the drug's efficacy.[6] To date, ABthrax has been developed entirely with private funds, but in order to move forward the company needs a commitment from the federal government to develop,

---

[5] Press Release, The White House, President Details Project BioShield, (Feb. 3, 2003) (http://www.whitehouse.gov/news/releases/2003/02/20030203.html).

[6] Under the Bioterrorism Act of 2002, the FDA specified the evidence required to demonstrate the efficacy of new drug and biological products used to counter biological agents, when traditional efficacy studies in humans are not feasible. Public Health Security And Bioterrorism Preparedness And Response Act Of 2002: Section 123. http://www.fda.gov/oc/bioterrorism/PL107-188.html. According to the guidelines set forth in the Act, successful studies in relevant animal models will be considered sufficient to establish efficacy for licensure and marketing approval. ABthrax is effective in preventing anthrax infection in two relevant models, rabbits and nonhuman primates. According to the guidelines, human clinical trials will be required to establish safety, tolerability, and pharmacology, but not efficacy.

manufacture and purchase the drug. With sufficient government support, Human Genome Sciences can begin producing significant quantities of ABthrax by the end of next year.

While the Department of Health and Human Services currently has the authority to purchase and stockpile drugs such as ABthrax, the specific framework created by Project BioShield would clarify and enhance that authority. Indeed, overlapping jurisdictions between HHS and the Department of Homeland Security have complicated the picture. A defined and transparent process – with a clear path between threat evaluation, scientific validation and product procurement – will go a long way toward giving companies the assurance they need to develop innovative new products to protect the public from chemical or biological attacks.

1200 G Street NW, Suite 400
Washington, DC 20005-3814
Tel: 202 783 8700
Fax: 202 783 8750
www.AdvaMed.org

Record

AdvaMed
Advanced Medical Technology Association

Statement for the Record

by

The Advanced Medical Technology Association (AdvaMed)

Government Reform Committee

Hearing on
Project BioShield: Contracting for the Health and Security of the American Public

Friday, April 4, 2003

AdvaMed
Advanced Medical Technology Association

AdvaMed, the Advanced Medical Technology Association, is pleased to submit this statement for the record before the Government Reform Committee. AdvaMed supports Project Bioshield and appreciates the Committee's attention to this important initiative. In addition, we hope the Committee will consider the important ways the medical device industry can partner with the government to help fight against bioterrorism and other threats to public health.

AdvaMed appreciated the opportunity to testify at the recent joint hearing of the Energy and Commerce Health Subcommittee and the Homeland Security Committee on Project Bioshield. On behalf of AdvaMed, Dr. Gary Noble, Vice President for Medical and Public Health Affairs and former expert on infectious diseases at the Centers for Disease Control and Prevention, was invited to testify on the integral role medical devices play in detecting and diagnosing exposure to bioterrorist agents, as well as treating those exposed and delivering needed vaccines to patients.

AdvaMed represents more than 1,100 innovators and manufacturers of medical devices, diagnostic products and medical information systems. Our members produce nearly 90 percent of the $75 billion in health care technology products consumed annually in the United States and nearly 70 percent of $170 billion purchased around the world annually. Many of these technologies – such as rapid tests to diagnose diseases caused by bioterrorism, gels and foams that can rapidly close wounds, bioengineered skin products for burn victims, and information systems to communicate critical public health information – form an important part of a timely, effective response to terrorist attacks.

AdvaMed's Medical Technology Preparedness Council

In response to the events of September 11, 2001, AdvaMed established the Medical Technology Preparedness Council to assist federal agencies in ensuring that the health care delivery system is fully prepared. The Council, established in October 2001, meets regularly to discuss issues and concerns, and has begun to work with key government preparedness entities including the Office of Emergency Preparedness (OEP), the Secretary's Command Center, the Food and Drug Administration (FDA), the Metropolitan Medical Response System (MMRS), and with individuals at the Centers for Disease Control and Prevention (CDC) who were administering the Strategic National Stockpile, among others.

We strongly support the principle of a public-private partnership in the area of preparedness. AdvaMed sponsored a sold-out conference on February 6, entitled "Innovation for Preparedness: the Public-Private Partnership," to strengthen the partnership between the government and the private sector on preparedness and to connect medical technology innovators with appropriate federal preparedness entities. Representatives from key preparedness entities within the federal government, including OEP, CDC, FDA, the Department of Defense, the National Institute of Allergy and Infectious Diseases (NIAID), the Department of Defense, the U.S. Army Medical Research Institute of Infectious Disease (USAMRIID) and the Environmental Protection Agency participated in the conference.

AdvaMed
Advanced Medical Technology Association

Medical Technology: Key to Rapid and Effective Response

Many of the technologies our companies manufacture or are developing are integral to a rapid and effective response to any potential terrorist attack, including among others:

- **Diagnostic Tests:** In November 2001, Roche Diagnostics and the Mayo Clinic announced the development of a new rapid anthrax test that can detect anthrax in humans in an hour and quickly made the test available to public health agencies and hospital and reference laboratories. Companies are working to develop diagnostic tests for other bioterrorist infectious agents, including smallpox. AdvaMed and its companies are also working cooperatively with FDA and the CDC to speed development of a diagnostic test for West Nile virus.

- **Vaccine and Drug Delivery Devices:** "Microdelivery" devices in development by BD will deliver vaccines more efficiently and effectively, allowing better absorption by the body and at the same time extending vaccine supply. For example, in collaboration with USAMRIID, researchers have shown that use of these skin-based microdelivery technologies can significantly improve the performance of next-generation recombinant protein vaccines against anthrax and the organism that causes toxic shock.

- **Biochemical Decontamination Technologies:** We saw the importance of technologies to decontaminate large contained areas and their contents, sensitive electronic equipment, mail and other items after the anthrax attacks of 2001. STERIS Corporation and the U.S. Army Edgewood Chemical Biological Center have entered into a collaborative research and development project to evaluate, optimize and modify STERIS's Vaporized Hydrogen Peroxide (VHP®) technology and to demonstrate its effectiveness against biological and chemical warfare agents.

- **Blood Safety Technologies:** Companies continue to work on technologies to protect our blood supply through inactivation or pathogen removal technology to inactivate or eliminate blood-borne viruses, parasites, lymphocytes and bacteria from blood products.

- **Advanced Burn and Wound Care Technologies:** Companies have developed gels and foams that can rapidly close wounds and bioengineered skin for the treatment of second and third degree burns. On September 11th 2001, Smith and Nephew, Inc. employees personally drove bioengineered skin products to New York City and Washington, D.C. to ensure patient access to these critical technologies despite the disruption to the distribution and supply chains because of U.S. airspace closures.

AdvaMed
Advanced Medical Technology Association

- **Health Information Systems:** Coordination of information by local, state and national public health authorities is key for managing efficient immunization activities and detecting biological outbreaks. Specialized vaccination tracking systems being developed by BD and others can help document and manage adverse events to vaccines while assuring rapid, safe vaccine deployment. As a measure of the critical role health information systems can play, last Friday, the Department of Health and Human Services (HHS) announced that it will begin testing a system using handheld personal digital assistants (PDAs) for transmitting urgent information about biological agents to clinicians. The three-month pilot test is designed to gauge the best ways for federal officials to communicate effectively with front-line clinicians in the event of a bioterrorist attack.

- **Basic Medical Technologies:** Basic medical technologies are also essential during times of crisis including ventilators, imaging technologies and infusion and monitoring equipment among others as well as gowns, gloves, masks and respirators to protect health care workers. A November 2001 *JAMA* article co-authored by Anthony S. Fauci, M.D. attributes the reduction in mortality in the inhalation anthrax cases to technological advances in diagnostics, imaging, microbiology, antibiotics and critical care.

AdvaMed Supports Project BioShield

AdvaMed strongly supports the Project BioShield initiative. Recent media reports confirm that some terrorist groups have the willingness to use bioterror agents and have been trying to develop the capability to launch infectious agents. Additionally, the rapidity of the global spread of severe acute respiratory syndrome (SARS) highlights the vulnerabilities we face.

Specifically, AdvaMed's Council supports provisions in Project BioShield that will:

- Speed research and development on biomedical countermeasures by streamlining current NIH processes and providing funding for the construction and improvement of facilities needed to safely support research and development of countermeasures;
- Provide necessary funding to purchase biomedical countermeasures for the stockpile particularly those countermeasures determined not to have commercial markets; and
- Allow the Secretary to make promising treatments available in an emergency, even for those products that do not yet have full FDA approval.

Project BioShield Should Include All Medical Technologies

AdvaMed
Advanced Medical Technology Association

Qualified Countermeasures. It is critical that *all* medical technologies – including devices, diagnostics and health information systems – be eligible for inclusion in all aspects of Project BioShield. The proposal submitted to Congress by the Administration provides significant discretionary authority for the Secretary of HHS to identify specific

AdvaMed
Advanced Medical Technology Association

countermeasures to threats that would be appropriate for procurement and for inclusion in the national stockpile. The Secretary must annually determine whether such countermeasures have a significant commercial market other than as homeland security countermeasures. The Secretary should have the clear authority to include all medical technologies in these determinations.

While many focus on vaccines as the sole countermeasures needed to counteract bioterror agents, as we saw with the inhalation anthrax cases and are seeing again with SARS, the ability to diagnose individuals to determine who has been exposed is essential to treatment and to limiting the contagious spread of infection. Additionally, in the case of the anthrax attacks in the Senate Hart Building, the Brentwood Postal facility and others, as manufacturers continue to develop rapid tests like the Roche-Mayo Clinic anthrax test, they hold the promise that many individuals will be able to forego prophylactic antibiotic or other treatment. And as diagnostic tests advance, we will be able to detect those who have been exposed and are infectious yet are not exhibiting any signs of illness -- as some are speculating is the possibility with SARS.

In the event of a bioterrorist attack, it will be critically important to ensure that all of the elements essential to treatment – diagnostic tests, specialized syringes and needles to deliver vaccines, information systems to assure safe and rapid vaccine deployment, and more -- are delivered along with the vaccines. We strongly recommend that in drafting BioShield legislation, the Congress extend to the Secretary the authority to consider *all* medical technologies, including devices, in determining what technologies are needed to protect our nation from potential bioterrorist events.

Medical Products for Use in Emergencies. The proposal submitted to Congress by the Administration would extend authority to the Secretaries of HHS and Defense to declare a national, public health or military emergency justifying the authorization of a drug or device if they determine that it may be effective in detecting, diagnosing, treating or preventing a serious or life-threatening condition. They must also determine that the known and potential benefits of the product outweigh the known and potential risks of the product and that there is no adequate, approved and available alternative.

The Secretaries should have the ability to consider all medical technologies for use in emergencies. For example, most diagnostic tests are reviewed through FDA's 510(k) process. A test approved to detect a specific bacterium or viral agent may be modified to detect another bacterium or virus of the same family. FDA's 510(k) process recognizes that diagnostic test development is an iterative process that builds on the knowledge gained from the previous infectious agent to develop tests for similar agents. Thus, it is conceivable that a previously approved diagnostic test may also prove to be useful in screening some bioterrorist agents. The value of this process is not limited to diagnostic tests but is the mainstay of all 510(k) products.

We strongly recommend that the Congress draft legislation that is broadly inclusive of all medical technologies, including 510(k) products. In the event that a product might have a needed countermeasure application, it should not be excluded because of a technicality.

AdvaMed
Advanced Medical Technology Association

Need for Strong Liability Protections

AdvaMed encourages the inclusion of strong liability protections for all aspects of Project BioShield, including medical devices. Presumably, those products that are declared qualified countermeasures under Project BioShield would also be declared qualified anti-terrorism technologies under Section 861 of the Homeland Security Act and would thus be eligible for the liability protections of that Act. However, it is not clear that companies whose products are declared for use in national, public health or military emergency situations would be eligible for the Section 861 protections. Such products, by definition, have not yet been reviewed or approved for use by FDA. Liability concerns will be a key consideration for companies manufacturing both qualified countermeasures and emergency-use products and the legislation should make clear that the liability protections of Sec. 861 of the Homeland Security Act apply to such products.

Importance of Assuring Adequate Supplies in the Event of a Significant Attack

As Congress works on Project BioShield and assuring the availability of medical technologies to protect and treat patients, we also recommend that Congress be mindful of the problems that can arise during a crisis in getting these technologies to patients. In the wake of a significant attack or disaster, it will be necessary to ensure that local providers are adequately supplied with appropriate medical equipment to care for casualties. As part of the AdavMed's preparedness efforts, we have invested significant time and resources in working with the appropriate federal authorities to ensure that the needed medical materials and supplies will be available.

There is a critical initial period of 12-24 hours during which most supplies will come from local stocks in hospitals, other health care facilities, and local distributors. However, after that initial period, there will be a need to resupply these facilities. Local planners in particular seem to take the approach that "if it is needed, it will appear." AdvaMed has worked with Office of Emergency Preparedness and MMRS regarding the logistics of moving medical supplies to the scene of a major attack. Our objective has been to make planners at all levels aware of the issues around resupply and to provide advice about who to contact for resupply.

AdvaMed has worked closely with related trade associations, the Health Industry Distributors Association (HIDA) and the Association for Healthcare Resources and Materials Management (AHRMM) to develop a planning guide for state and local emergency planners that explains medical supply chains and logistics. The guide is currently being printed and details are being worked out for the physical distribution to members of the National Emergency Management Association (NEMA), the Association of State and Territorial Health Officials (ASTHO), and the National Association of City and County Health Officials (NACCHO). A prototype of this booklet is attached for your information.

AdvaMed
Advanced Medical Technology Association

AdvaMed has also supported the efforts of the AHRMM, HIDA and the Health Industry Group Purchasing Association (HIGPA) in the development of supply formularies. The formularies, which vary depending on whether the incident is chemical, biological, radiological, explosive, etc., are intended to act as a benchmark for emergency supply preparedness. They can be customized to meet the individual needs of hospitals and the communities they serve.

AdvaMed is also concerned about "business continuity" and the potential vulnerability of certain sites that monitor manufacture critical medical supplies. These sites may be the sole source for certain supplies. If these sites are incapacitated for whatever reason, critical supplies essential to quality health care may not be available. Ways to address this dilemma include establishment of alternative site manufacturing capacity as well as stockpiling additional inventory. We recommend that Congress consider this issue and that the Department of Homeland Security's Office of Information Analysis and Infrastructure Protection be charged with examining solutions that would provide incentives for industry to create back-up capacity or such other solutions as may be appropriate, including use of the Strategic National Stockpile.

Conclusion

We thank the Chairman for holding this hearing and hope the Committee will keep in mind the important role medical devices can and will play in fighting bioterrorism and other threats to public health. During this time of national crisis, the Medical Technology Preparedness Council stands ready to work with the federal government to achieve our mutual goals of defending the homeland from terrorist attacks and providing the best medical care possible for our citizens. We also look forward to working with the Committee to assure the enactment of BioShield legislation consistent with this testimony.

APEX
TP
9780160704147
76901945 – 29